VISIONS OF UTOPIA

VISIONS OF UTOPIA

Edward Rothstein

Herbert Muschamp

Martin E. Marty

The New York Public Library

OXFORD
UNIVERSITY PRESS

2003

OXFORD
UNIVERSITY PRESS

Oxford   New York
Auckland   Buenos Aires   Cape Town   Chennai
Dar es Salaam   Delhi   Hong Kong   Istanbul   Karachi
Kolkata Kuala Lumpur   Madrid   Melbourne   Mexico City
Mumbai Nairobi   São Paulo   Shanghai   Taipei   Tokyo   Toronto

Copyright © 2003 Oxford University Press, Inc.
Published by Oxford University Press, Inc.
198 Madison Avenue, New York, New York 10016
www.oup.com

Oxford is a registered trademark of Oxford University Press

Library of Congress Cataloging-in-Publication Data

Rothstein, Edward,1952-
Visions of utopia/Edward Rothstein, Herbert Muschamp, Martin E. Marty
p. cm.
ISBN 0-19-514461-9
1. Utopias
I. Muschamp, Herbert.
II. Marty, Martin E., 1928-
III. Title.
HX806 .R595 2002
335'.02—dc212002010396

10 9 8 7 6 5 4 3 2 1
Printed in the United States of America
on acid-free paper

CONTENTS

VISIONS OF UTOPIA

INTRODUCTION

THE THREE ESSAYS THAT COMPRISE THIS BOOK WERE ORIGINALLY PRESENTED AS separate lectures in the 2000 Oxford University Press/New York Public Library lecture series. In that year, with the millennium approaching, the topic of utopia seemed an appropriate one to explore. The Library mounted a major exhibition entitled "Utopia: The Search for the Ideal Society in the Western World." Oxford invited a trio of distinguished speakers—the cultural critic Edward Rothstein, the architecture critic Herbert Muschamp, and the historian of religion Martin E. Marty—to discuss the history of utopian thought, its incarnations, and implications. The result is three distinct yet related pieces which remind their readers of the range of writers, artists, and religious thinkers who have concerned themselves with the search for an ideal human society, and what we can learn from their ideas and experiences.

In the first essay, Edward Rothstein examines what might be called the tragedy of utopia, the essential fact that any utopian project contains the seed of its own destruction, whether in violent revolution, totalitarianism, or mere intolerance. Yet he also illuminates the inextricable link between an underlying belief in utopian ideals—harmony, equality, the elimination of unmet needs or desire, ethical interaction, and the resulting potential for new forms of human consciousness—and the very possibility of social progress. Whatever the dangers of utopian efforts, Rothstein argues that "the quest itself" is still an imaginative precondition for achievable change in the here and now. He uses the nascent technology of the Internet as an illustration of a quasi-utopian project—one that may never bring about the complete erasure of conventional identities and forms of interaction which its creators imagined, but which has nevertheless altered social relations in our existing world in fundamental ways.

Herbert Muschamp finds the utopian impulse, in this case defined as a wholeness derived from the desire to integrate the opposite or the disparate, in two seemingly different human endeavors. In his view, architecture and the practice of Buddhism are brought together by their similar dependence upon the continual interrogation and refinement of perception. Architects such as Adolph Loos wrestle with the utopian ideal by designing buildings that mediate between esthetic and social demands, between the inner space of the building and the outer space of its context. The cosmology of Mahayana Buddhism, based on the metaphorical understanding that the eventual perfection of the lotus flower depends upon the murky disorder of the swamp—the only environment in which it can grow—seeks to realize utopian possibility through a deep understanding of opposition and paradox. Such understanding, in Muschamp's view, fosters an engagement with the world that recognizes imperfection by continually seeking to refine perception of subjective experience and objective reality, and thereby creating the possibility of transcendence.

In the final essay Martin E. Marty discusses three historical examples of utopian thought that are crucial to our understanding of it: Thomas More's *Utopia*, theologian Thomas Müntzer's effort to build a community centered on his religious principles in sixteenth-century Germany, and the community imagined by another German religious thinker, Johann Valentine Andreae, in his seventeenth-century work *Christianoplis*. If Rothstein reminds us that utopian programs are intrinsically doomed to failure, Marty suggests we view attempts to realize a perfect society with "humane irony." For Marty, the greatest value of utopian thought is found in the balance between an understanding of its recognition of human potential and a healthy skepticism for the absolute order that most utopias ultimately envision.

At once eclectic and far-reaching, these essays taken together speak powerfully to the complexity and the paradox inherent in the search for the perfect world, and the ways in which the notion of utopia challenges the boundaries of human imagination.

Furaha D. Norton

VISIONS OF UTOPIA

UTOPIA AND ITS DISCONTENTS

Edward Rothstein

AND IT SHALL COME TO PASS, IN THE END OF DAYS, THAT RIVERS OF MILK AND nectar shall flow, that the wolf shall dwell with the lamb and spears shall be beaten into pruning hooks, that philosophers shall be kings, that there will be no hypocrisy, dissembling, deceit, flattery, strife, or discord. There shall be neither hate nor envy nor hunger nor thirst. There shall be much leisure and few lawyers. There shall be no private property, and there shall be communal camaraderie. From each shall come work according to his abilities and to each shall come support according to his needs. New forms of human consciousness will evolve. Our erotic natures will be freed from gratuitous repression, and society will bask in polymorphous redemption. Neither shall we learn war anymore. And all of us, both great and small, shall know bliss.

Sure.

Yet all of this has been promised. This utopia was described by Ovid, anticipated in medieval tales of Cockaigne, named by Thomas More, predicted by Karl Marx, satirized by Samuel Butler, popularly imagined by Edward Bellamy, heralded by Marcuse and B. F. Skinner and Teilhard de Chardin, championed by contemporary Internet enthusiasts and hackers—this land has changed remarkably little over the millennia. It remains, as it was when More named it in the sixteenth century, utopia—meaning "no place." And while each of these imagined paradises was indeed *some*place, they might as well not have been. They are found across unmapped oceans, like More's no-place, or high atop mountains, like H. G. Wells's utopia, or found buried in the arcana of esoteric mystical writings of the Kabbalists, or envisioned in the dialectical musings of Hegel and Marx, or nestled in the Himalayas like Shangri-La of the popular novel and movie *Lost Horizon*.

They are so distant, so beyond ordinary life, that very few people actually get to experience paradise in person. In almost every case, the vision of this perfect world must come to us through a pilgrim who stumbles upon the hidden utopia by accident or weird novelistic device: perhaps falling asleep in a mesmeric trance for 120 years, like Bellamy's hero in *Looking Backward*. Even when the utopia is sought rather than stumbled upon, the quest for it involves a suspension of normal life. The journey to utopia is also full of dangers. Plato showed again and again how the philosopher, seeking the illumination of the sun, must descend back into the darkness of the cave and wrestle with those of us who reject his supposed enlightenment, greeting him with the same sort of skepticism I am expressing toward utopian accounts of pilgrims' progress. And why should anybody else believe the vision when not even the messenger bringing the good news can quite believe what he has seen? Typically, the prophet, witness, visitor, or seeker is himself shocked by the scope of the utopian vision and has to be gradually inducted into its strange ways by a native, who conveniently provides anthropological lectures on how strife and envy are eliminated and plenty and pleasures are ensured.

These utopias, difficult to reach, difficult to believe in, and difficult to tell about, might seem to be unreachable fantasies or make-believe kingdoms. But the entire point of the utopia genre is not to reveal perfectly unreachable worlds like Peter Pan's Neverland, with its boyhood fantasies, or Tolkien's Lothlorien, with its dreamlike forest glades and elfin rulers. Utopia is not an impossible place, or at any rate, it is generally not *supposed* to be. It is a place that can conceivably exist—and, in the teller's view, a place that *should* exist. At any rate, however out of reach, most utopias are meant to be pursued. Utopias represent an ideal toward which the mundane world must reach. They are examples to be worked for. Utopianism creates a political program, giving direction and meaning to the idea of progress; progress is always on the way toward some notion of utopia.

There are, of course, complicated undercurrents in all this. Some imagined visions of utopias are partly satirical; no one, for example, has ever been sure how much of More's vision was meant to be ironic. Some utopias are also often critical rather than affirmative, invoking the earthly elements of greed and envy and inequality, only to suggest that if the correct strategies are followed, they might be overcome or avoided. But utopias, properly interpreted, are visions of what *should* be, even if they show what *shouldn't* be. Utopias are visions we care about because they have implications for *this* world; they are attempts to say what this world could be and what should be worked for.

But what if utopia is not imagined as an ideal to be sought elsewhere, but as something real to be sought here and now? There are books that imagine what happens when the utopia isn't a mythical no-place, but a transformation of this-place. When Aldous Huxley imagined a genetically engineered and drugged society, for example, or George Orwell imagined constellations of totalitarian power and the elimination of private life, they were not imagining worlds in which the inhabitants generally considered themselves unhappy or stifled. *Brave New World* and *1984* do not show societies designed to create unhappiness. These societies were specifically designed by their rulers in order to be *utopias,* not *dystopias.* They were established, of course, to consolidate absolute power, but they could do so only by creating the most stable society possible, the greatest contentment distributed among the largest number of people. And indeed, for many citizens of these lands the utopian project succeeds. For the satisfied citizens, no better society can be imagined, and none could more skillfully manage human desires and needs. These are utopias that have come to pass, presumably in our own world. And that turns out to be the problem, for all of these paradises are really varieties of hell.

This suggests that one man's utopia is another man's dystopia. Utopias seem fine if they are far-off and protected realms; bring them any closer and they easily turn sour. What is one actually to do in utopia? What sort of life is possible when all desires are satisfied? In the monotonous world of utopias, distinctions and judgments become difficult to make; virtue and horror run together. There is no private property in More's utopia, just as there is no private world in *1984*. There is total devotion to the stability of the nation in Bellamy's utopia, just as there is in *Brave New World*. Pick a virtue and watch it turn into vice. For Plato, for example, the defining principle of his republic was justice. A just state would be like a just soul, each part in balance with the other, each part serving the whole by being most true to itself: the warriors, the laborers, and the philosophers—all with a role—each contributing to the harmony of the state. For Bellamy, More, and many others, right up until the present, the defining principle is egalitarianism. If all citizens are equal—rights, property, privilege—then all sources of envy and conflict are eliminated; desires are satisfied because no unreasonable desires develop. But don't these ideals of justice and equality also have the potential of creating social hells? In one, isn't there the risk of creating rivalrous clans demanding justice or rejecting the philosophical roles mapped out for them? In the other, isn't there a risk of increasing regimentation to prevent eruptions of desire and ambition? Look closely at Edward Bellamy's vision of the American future, published in 1888, and it seems like an ideological glorification of the Soviet Union in the 1930s. The government is an all-powerful corporation; citizens divide all profits equally, and their loyalty is guaranteed through the strict military discipline of an "industrial army." There are communal kitchens and laundry rooms offered in scrupulously egalitarian housing. Incentives for high achievement in industry consist of miniature medals of bronze, silver, and gold that somehow suffice to spur ambition without creating envy. Look too closely at this utopia or any other, and one begins to shiver at the possibility. The last century's worst horrors—including Nazi Germany, the Soviet regime, the Maoist Cultural Revolution—grew out of utopian visions. With such examples in mind, the philosopher Isaiah Berlin argued that utopianism leads to not to freedom but to tyranny. He regularly invoked Kant in reproof: "Out of the crooked timber of humanity, no straight thing was ever made." The philosopher Karl Popper, in *The Open Society and Its Enemies* (which he began writing in 1938, on the day the Nazis invaded Austria), wrote that those who envision making "heaven on earth" will only succeed in making it hell.

This is, then, a very peculiar situation. There are indeed ideals represented in utopias, ideals that shape our notions of progress. Utopias implicitly provide a standard by which we judge our political and social achievements. But what sorts of standards are these? How closely can they be reconciled with what we know of the world? Are they even worthy as models? Consider again the idea of a perfect society, in which material plenty joins with social harmony. Imagine somehow that nature, in all its unpredictable irrationality, were temporarily willing to cooperate with this fantasy by providing plentiful rainfall and sunshine in their proper times and places. Imagine that the infinite variety of human personality and the arbitrary reach of human desire could somehow be accommodated. Imagine that unhappiness could really be an occasional occurrence, worthy of note because it gives a more potent awareness of happiness. In such a world, where everything else seemed to be going right, we would still have to believe that people really are, as academic critical theory now insists, socially constructed, that everything that we like and believe, every way that we act and think, is shaped by our surroundings and institutions, that there is no aspect of human nature that might serve as an obstacle to an engineered paradise. And even if we were ready to grant such a notion of near-infinite human malleability—something for which there is no credible evidence—we would still run into a contradiction. For surely liberty and freedom would seem to be aspects of life one would not want to do without in any utopia. Yet also, in any utopia, there would have to be a very strong central authority. Without such an authority, how could social construction and constructed harmony be guaranteed? The famed maxim of Marx and Engels—"from each according to his abilities, to each according to his needs"—is, for example, a noble idea. We contribute what we are able and in return are provided what we reasonably require. But who measures these abilities or decides whether or not they are being suitably used? And who determines needs and how they might vary from time to time and place to place? Only a centralized authority could enforce such an ideal. Under a weak government—or even one only a bit sloppy in its vigilance—the categorization of abilities and needs would come under question. Slight variations would creep in. One citizen might read utopian fiction and come to believe that there are better ways to organize an ideal society. Another might suddenly develop a strong taste for artichoke hearts and be willing to sacrifice a good deal to eat them out of season. The unpredictable is one of the predictable aspects in human associations. Yet the unpredictable is just what a utopia is unprepared for—which is one reason why these tightly regulated societies seem plausible only in small communities in social isolation. Almost any utopia seems to make one very clear demand: obey. Utopians know best. Even the ordinary family would pose a threat to utopia because it would seem to create loyalties that might supersede those demanded by the state. Private proper-ty would have to be eliminated, or there would be lawsuits over its disposition and envy over its possession. The more perfect the utopia, the more stringent must be the controls. We are left with, yes, Big Brother. And utopia becomes totalitarianism with a barely human face.

Is this, perhaps, one reason for the distinct uneasiness that some-times accompanies utopian writing? A utopia is like one of those for-bidden gardens in fairy tales, hidden from view by briars and ringed with thorns, or surrounded by flames like the sleeping body of Brünnhilde; it often seems that even if one were to gain admittance, there would be a high price to pay. Literary utopias are also fraught with ambiguity, as if nothing could quite be what it seems. More's *Utopia* is a resolutely secular society, a peculiar paradise to have been created by a representative of the Church; this and other aspects of the book have led some to suggest that at times More is showing not a utopia but what a utopia should *not* be. Samuel Butler's *Erewhon*, a satire of utopian literature, also presents its share of ambiguities; in Erewhon, for example, criminals are considered to be ill and are treated for their illness. What an enlightened idea for the late nineteenth century, one might think, except for the fact that in Butler's utopia the satire runs deep: Criminals must be treated for illness, but anyone treated for illness must also be imprisoned.

The closer one looks, the more ambiguity there is. Moreover, what is in question is not only utopia's virtue but also the procedures required to reach it. Utopia stands outside of history. It is the city on the hill, society's dream image. But it can be reached only by breaking the continuity of history. Any attempt to really create a utopia is necessarily revolutionary. The manners, morals, and convictions of the past have to be cast aside. The realization of a utopia requires destruction. Like the French Revolution, a passage into utopia would involve the creation of a new calendar and a new law; like the French Revolution, too, it would require a certain price to be paid in blood.

Let me give an example other than the obvious political ones of the previous century. Utopianism is closely related to the notion of messianism, the idea that there is a figure, a messiah, who will bring about the utopia. He is the messenger who brings the good news down to earth and then helps put it into effect. He comes from outside history, enters into its midst, and promises redemption. These are borders that are transgressed only with great trauma, which is why so many heralds of messianic days are associated with cataclysm and apocalypse. The end of days is literally the end of time.

One of the most extreme and unusual examples of messianism's cataclysmic consequences came in the seventeenth century. At that time, in the Mediterranean lands and the Middle East, a nondescript, slightly manic, and oddly disturbed man proclaimed himself the Messiah of the Jews. In a magisterial essay, "Redemption Through Sin," the historian of Jewish mysticism Gershom Scholem recounted how this mentally unbalanced man, Sabbatai Zevi, engaged in rather bizarre acts—marrying a prostitute, mocking sacred texts, even instituting a new blessing, praising "that which is forbidden." A devoted Kabbalist of the time became his "prophet," interpreting these acts and other violations of Jewish law according to Kabbalistic mythology. According to this messianic theory, Sabbatai Zevi was not perverse or crazy. He was actually seeking sparks of divinity, which were deeply hidden even in what was most forbidden; he had to free those sparks from their polluting "husks" and restore them to their divine origins. His acts of sin were actually acts of redemption.

Eventually, Scholem pointed out, Sabbateanism became a staggeringly popular movement (Isaac Bashevis Singer imagined some of its consequences in his first novel, *Satan in Goray*). Carried to its logical conclusion, the idea of descent into the netherworld in order to free divine sparks from polluting husks led to the very sanctification of transgression; it was a declaration of the holiness of sin. Then, just as matters of doctrine seemed settled, the Turkish sultan, nervous about the upheaval among the Jews, called Sabbatai before him and gave him a choice: convert to Islam or be put to death. Sabbatai may have been crazy, but he wasn't that crazy. The conversion took place. It was, Scholem explained, a cataclysm for those who believed. How could such a savior so completely abandon his mission? Yet even that shock did not immediately invalidate the messianic expectations; the conversion too could be interpreted as a "descent" that would lead to salvation. But eventually, Scholem suggests, there was a widespread crisis that put the entire religious tradition into question, sowing the seeds of the secular Enlightenment.

Sabbatai Zevi, of course, was an extreme case. He didn't just declare the end of earthly and religious law, he heralded its inversion—deliberate violation. But in descending into transgression, in cultivating sin, he demonstrated a typical consequence of attempts to create utopias. He dramatized what is involved in every utopia: The mundane must be overturned, the future paradise will have nothing to do with earthly history or its familiar order. Messianic revolutions—like the French Revolution, which followed Sabbatean patterns—usually institute new calendars, to signify the beginning of a new era, leaving behind the old. Messianism, in its promise to redeem history, ends up violating history. Scholem called messianism a "theory of catastrophe." So, it seems, is utopianism, particularly when utopianism is treated as something to be practically worked for and imminently expected. It is astonishing how much violation a utopian will tolerate and even celebrate.

Lenin in 1917 offers another extreme example: "Until the 'higher phase' of communism arrives," he wrote, "the Socialists demand the *strictest* control, by society and *by the state,* of the measure of labor and the measure of consumption; but this control must start with the expropriation of the capitalists, with the establishment of workers' control over the capitalists, and must be carried out, not by a state of bureaucrats, but by a state of *armed workers.*" In the name of higher hopes, Lenin, prefiguring Stalin, cautions, "We do not in the least deny the possibility and the inevitability of excesses." But with the removal of the first cause of oppression—the capitalist system— even such excesses will "wither away."

This is catastrophic messianism: Redemption can take place only through a long march through the netherworld of accidental excesses and planned destruction. The Nazis, masters of the underworld, differed only in superstructure. The strategy was the same: In the name of future glory, what will not be permissible? Utopias stand apart from history; their realization demands Sabbateanism.

So let us put aside such extremes and look not at these intellectual and literary fantasies we call utopias but at something far more important: the quest itself, the belief that something perfect is possible, utopianism itself. The discontents of utopianism have subtle ramifications that affect almost all forms of contemporary political debate. The issues were discussed by Lionel Trilling in his 1950 book *The Liberal Imagination*. One of the great achievements of modern times, in Trilling's view, was the development of political liberalism: the view that there were universal and inalienable human rights and that the powers of reason could both honor those rights and ameliorate the world's evils. This is not a utopian belief; it is a humanitarian and practical one. It grows out of experience, it acknowledges ambiguity and complication, and it refuses to seek perfection. This kind of liberalism, which has now become the unspoken premise for most mainstream political discussion in this country, does not believe in absolutes; it believes in accommodation and adjustment.

But even liberalism is not free from utopian risk. Trilling points out that the moment liberalism decides to take action against ills—that is, to try to accomplish something systematic in society—it requires organization, legislation, documentation, justification. It encourages bureaucratic qualities of mind that in the extreme case could lead to a variety of Stalinism and in the mildest case could lead to a stifling accumulation of regulations and restrictions. The desire to reshape the world according to an ideal, Trilling suggests, requires a readiness to accept a simplified view of the mind and the world, and an unwavering conviction about how they might be shaped. It does not require—indeed, does not consider relevant—the inner life, with all its contradictory passions and intricate musings. It cannot, if it seeks its ideal, accept the kinds of complication and character that Trilling celebrated in the nineteenth-century novel. This blindness to the fullness of the human spirit, in Trilling's view, is why liberalism always risks becoming illiberal. So the enlargement of freedom risks the contraction of freedom. "Some paradox of our natures," Trilling writes, "leads us, when once we have made our fellow men the objects of our enlightened interest, to go on to make them the objects of our pity, then of our wisdom, ultimately of our coercion." Such are the dangers of the utopian impulse in liberalism.

This also, Trilling suggests, alters cultural life. In order to believe that society can be rationally organized to create the greatest good for the greatest number, the human mind must be transformed. The inner life must shrink, deferring to the material world. All dark desires, untamable impulses, ambivalent feelings, and rabid thoughts would then be considered not as inescapable products of the human mind but as stemming from the failings of the world, from imperfections in the social order. So liberalism risks yet another distortion, its compassionate understanding evolving into doctrinaire puritanism and a simplified view of humanity.

This is liberalism's great temptation, in Trilling's view—an understanding he shared with Isaiah Berlin. "Life presses us so hard," he writes, "time is so short, the suffering of the world is so huge, simple, unendurable—anything that complicates our moral fervor in dealing with reality as we immediately see it and wish to drive head-long upon it must be regarded with some impatience." Liberalism, like utopianism, is, in its adversary position toward the world, a trans-forming force, and a noble endeavor; it is also, in its adversary posi-tion toward the complexities of the mind with all its ambiguities and conflicts, a force that places limits on the human. Trilling found sim-ilar tension in the peculiar nature of American democracy, which distrusted the very powers of mind it relied upon, objecting to the ways the mind created limits to freedom, creating order and hierar-chy, insisting on boundaries and conditions. There is no simple resolution to these tensions. Any notion of social progress is going to flirt with illiberal and doctrinaire simplification. This is the shadow cast by utopianism even on the most flexible and rational vision of human society. But without that vision, without a liberal understand-ing of the possibilities of human nature, we will be just as lost. There is a tragic quality to these tensions.

What is the answer, then? A rejection of all expectation of improve-ment? An abandonment of all ideals? The tendency of conservatism to look backward for a historical restoration is no greater help. Conservativism too can be a variety of utopianism, with its own dangers enshrining an unchangeable and inhuman Golden Age. At stake is real-ly a different view of human nature. Liberals view it as malleable, read-ily reshaped by social change; conservatives consider human nature to be relatively immutable, in fact stubbornly so, resistant to ideas about how things should or could be. Liberals envision potential equality; con-servatives are resigned to (and in extreme cases celebrate) inequality. Bellamy, for example, in his liberal vision of an egalitarian future, shows how desires, expectations, venality, and envy have all evaporated under the pressure of social reform. A conservative would reject this possibility of total egalitarianism and envision an inevitably dark future in which poverty and vice survive as constant challenges. The American conservative ideal of "equality of opportunity" means that some will be able to thrive and others will not. In fact, the conservative government is about as far from the utopian government as you can get. The ideal is to govern the least, in confidence that however many complications and conflicts may arise, the aspirations of the many will distribute good to all but the fewest few.

But whatever the political position, whatever balance is established between unchanging nature and ever-changing culture, some view of an unreachable ideal seems unavoidable. The sociologist Karl Mannheim, in his now classic book *Ideology and Utopia*, argued that "the complete disappearance of the utopian element from human thought and action would mean that human nature and human development would take on a totally new character." He concluded: "With the relinquishment of utopias, man would lose his will to shape history, and therewith his ability to change it." The Danish philosopher Søren Kierkegaard also cherished that form of will: "If I could wish for something, I would wish for neither wealth nor power, but the passion of possibility; I would wish only for an eye which, eternally young, eternally burns with the longing to see possibility." His desire is not to lose the desire, to retain the ability to see that things could be different. This is not the same as wanting to see how inadequate things are when compared with the ideal.

It is difficult now, at the dawn of the twenty-first century, to say whether we have too much utopianism or too little. Utopianism enjoyed a resurgence in the 1960s and 1970s and still has its adherents, but many of those experiences led to disillusionment. Is there even any widespread conviction now that there is such a thing as progress? As a result of such disillusionment, there has even arisen a bit of nostalgia for the utopian spirit, perhaps reflected in this lecture series. What is missed is the conviction that some process exists that could dependably improve the human condition, even if the exile from Eden doesn't come to a complete end. It may be that the most challenging political question in a world appropriately wary of utopianism is how to envision progress without envisioning a utopia.

These questions are so vexed in the political arena that it may help to consider them briefly in two other realms that have come to play a large role in contemporary notions of progress and paradise: technology and culture. Both are suffused with utopian ideals. During the last two decades, in fact, technology almost became a repository for utopian energies. Technology, after all, is the art of transforming society through invention. Every great technological change has also led to social change. The railroad, the telegraph, the automobile, even the air conditioner altered conditions and expectations. David F. Noble, a historian at York University, pointed out in *The Religion of Technology: The Divinity of Man and the Spirit of Invention* that the "technological enterprise" is not a reflection of rationalist science but has always been "an essentially religious endeavor." Monasteries were centers of the mechanical arts. The English scientist Robert Boyle wrote a treatise entitled *Some Physico-Theological Considerations About the Possibility of the Resurrection*. Charles Babbage—the father of the modern computer—believed that advances in the "mechanical arts" provide "some of the strongest arguments in favor of religion." Noble also points out: "Masons have

been among the most prominent pioneers of every American transportation revolution: canals (Clinton and Van Rensselaer); steam-
boats (Robert Fulton); railroads (George Pullman, Edward Harriman,
James J. Hill); the automobile (Henry Ford); the airplane (Charles
Lindbergh), and space flight (at least half a dozen astronauts)." This
fits with the heritage of Masonry, with all its mysterious aura of
secret allegiances and rights: the ancient Masons were, supposedly,
the builders of the Temple, the architects of spiritual communication,
the first technologists of the spirit.

   Much technological innovation, in fact, is driven by a kind of utopianism: something new is introduced to the world that promises
transformation. Technology is disruptive, sometimes destructive, dis-
placing older procedures, products, and ideas. And with each change
comes the promise of further changes yet to come. Technology has
also been connected with a form of gnosticism, an almost mystical
attempt to purge illusion and reach true knowledge. Computer hackers use terms such as "deep magic" and "casting the runes" to
describe their craft. Virtual reality promises to break down the physical restraints of body and mind. There is a New Yorker cartoon
showing a household pet at a keyboard who turns to another four-
legged companion and explains, "On the Internet, nobody knows
you're a dog." On the Internet, many advocates have proclaimed, it
is possible to be anything, to dissolve all restrictions the material
world places on us. This spirit is also behind a revival of interest in
Marshall McLuhan, who thought of media as extensions of the body.
The alphabet, he argued, was a medium that turned tribal man into
modern man, imposing notions of reason and order. The electronic
media, he suggested in the days before the Internet, are doing the
opposite, creating a high-tech tribal culture in which literacy

becomes irrelevant. "I expect," McLuhan proclaimed, "to see the coming decades transform the planet into an art form: the new man, linked in a cosmic harmony that transcends time and space."

This vision of a new tribal man transformed by technology resonated with the utopian ideas of some participants in the 1960s counterculture who were pioneers in the development of the personal computer and the Internet. They consciously attempted to translate their visions into the new media. A few years ago, the critic Mark Dery suggested that the personal computer revolution could well be called "Counterculture 2.0." Dave Bunnell, an activist from SDS, founded *PC Magazine*. Steve Jobs created and promoted Apple as a countercultural computer. John Perry Barlow, a Grateful Dead lyricist and SDS activist, later became cofounder of the influential Electronic Frontier Foundation, an organization that was dedicated to preserving and expanding the libertarian terrain of the Internet. Stewart Brand, one of the creators of the *Whole Earth Catalog,* went on to found the Well— the Whole Earth 'Lectronic Link —in which veterans of a California commune helped build one of the first online communities. According to Theodor Roszak: "It was guerrilla computer hackers, whose origins can be discerned in the old *Whole Earth Catalog*, who invented the personal computer as a means, so they hoped, of fostering dissent and questioning authority." The odd thing in this technological culture has been the paradoxical mixture of an almost antirationalist, mystical temper together with the most advanced technological innovation.

There is even a recurring ritual that celebrates the Net culture's peculiar perspective as a tribal technocracy with messianic leanings. Every Labor Day weekend since 1986, a ceremony has taken place known as Burning Man. Each year over ten thousand celebrants, including motorcycle freaks, urban dropouts, thrill seekers, media professionals, and technology cultists, dress up in costumes, drive out to the Nevada desert, and erect a fifty-foot statue of a man. He is burned during the festival's final night. Kevin Kelly, a founder of *Wired* magazine, has called Burning Man "the holiday of choice for the digerati."

In this gathering, the digerati shed their usual hardware for turbans, masks, drag costumes, makeup, and Mad Max accessories mounted on automobiles. Human technology is on display; people are showing what they can make of themselves, proclaiming their liberation from constraints, declaring a new kind of social technology in which anything can be done or made. Technology has been displaced from metal to flesh; it is even celebrated—and destroyed —in flame.

A few years ago, at Nevada's Black Rock Desert, Larry Harvey, the event's impresario, addressed the fifteen-thousand-member audience: "Years ago, people asked me why the cybernetic people were coming out here, why the Internet people were coming out here, and I didn't have a clue 'cause I was still using a Bic pen. And gradually it dawned on me why they come out here. There's a great change coming over the world. These people have been inhabiting a world on the Internet which is non-hierarchic, radically democratic, essentially populist in character, in which you create your own reality and move where you want, and you wouldn't be judged for it. And they looked at this place and they said, 'Geez, that's an analog of cyber . . . that's cyberspace come true.' . . . You can be anybody on the Internet, and if you have an idea it will begin to pervade."

But one doesn't need to seek such ideas in the extremes of primitivistic ritual. Barlow, who is now one of the most established figures in Internet advocacy, wrote a "Declaration of the Independence of

Cyberspace" in 1996 to oppose any international attempt to create restrictions on Internet freedom. He declared the Internet "the new home of Mind" and chastised the "Governments of the Industrial World, you weary giants of flesh and steel": "Your legal concepts of property, expression, identity, movement, and context do not apply to us. They are based on matter. There is no matter here."

Kevin Kelly, who, as executive editor of *Wired* was one of the most influential early analysts of the Internet, recently wrote a.sort of self-help book for the Net-era businessperson, arguing that the idea of a computer network can help inspire a new form of business success that will help the planet progress. The new economy is a counter-cultural dream characterized by an "open society" with "decentral-ized ownership and equity" and "pools of knowledge instead of pools of capital." Generosity will beget wealth; the "swarm" will help the individual; "communication" will be more powerful than "com-putation." Though today these utopian ideas have been overshad-owed by our preoccupations with the crashes of dot-com business-es and Internet entertainments, it is difficult to underestimate the extent to which utopian ideas spurred the Internet's development in its early years. Utopianism animated enterprise and imagination, redefining the notion of technological progress.

But as in the social realm, problems come up when the utopian dream is treated as the model against which the real is sternly judged. The dangers in this case are not, as with so many other tech-nological innovations, that a Pandora's box is being opened; it is that the world itself is treated as if it must measure up to the fantasy. And this affects the development of policy. It caused the government to treat Internet access as if it would solve the problems of the public school classroom. In the mid-1990s President Clinton was planning to commit $10 billion for five years to wire schools—when actually, until the world's books are available online in digital form, a good library is better for many forms of research and learning.

Or consider the example of Napster—a brilliantly simple creation of a nineteen-year-old programmer that attracted $15 million in venture capital simply because it offered countless songs to Internet users without cost. In a variety of court cases, it claimed to be innocent of copyright violation, because of its elegant technological achievement. Napster was a middleman, allowing a user to download a song stored not on Napster's equipment but on another individual user's hard drive. Napster just arranged the match. Napster wasn't around for a long time, but the idea of Napster—using the Internet as a place for unregulated swapping of material—is going to develop, not disappear. Similar services continue to thrive.

The development of Napster and its more radical competitors is, of course, made possible by technological innovations. Mass piracy once meant that books had to be copied and bound; software had to be replicated and packaged; music had to be reproduced on professional machines. Now, in the digital domain, the costs of replication and distribution have dropped to nearly zero. There is no way to tell a copy from an original. Movies and books are going to be facing the same challenge as music. But the recurring justification for Napster-like activity comes out of the gnostic utopianism of the Internet pioneers: a suspicion of private property, a celebration of network effects and communal transmissions, a libertarian opposition to those who would rein in the tumult and draw boundaries on the electronic frontier. Barlow has argued that familiar notions of intellectual property become "towers of outmoded boilerplate" when applied to information on the Internet. Stewart Brand, whom I mentioned before, is credited with the phrase "Information wants to be free," a mantra that has become a rallying cry for challenges to copyright.

This romantic vision sees cyberspace as a realm fundamentally different from ordinary life. It has become increasingly difficult to separate this belief from important political and technological debates over copyright, privacy, and security. There is a hint of its influence, for example, in the Berkman Center for Internet and Society at Harvard University. Its Web site asserts that the Internet should foster new, "open" forms of governance and culture; important software code, they argue, should be available in the public domain; and a "countercopyright" sign, [cc], is encouraged to signal writers' willingness to allow copying and modification of their work. Some of the scholars involved in this movement have argued that the risk in cyberspace is not that copyright will be unrestricted—as Napster's opponents feared—but that it will be too radically restricted, that corporate control over reproduction and distribution could become so absolute that creativity will be stifled.

Concerns over privacy and control are not unjustified. Technology allows violations of privacy and propriety; health records, bank statements, and Internet use can all be accessed using the right tools. At the same time, information can be so rigorously controlled that free informalities of reading and listening can be put at risk. But the very same technology can also lead to an unprecedented amount of freedom. It allows communication across national boundaries, sharing of scholarly research, more efficient commerce, new forms of literary publication, and less expensive distribution of all arts. This mixture of violation and promise has been part of every shift in communications and technology.

The problem is that the Internet counterculture is preoccupied almost completely with a utopian idea of the Internet conceived when it was used by just a few tens of thousands of devotees and scientists; commerce was unforeseen and unwelcome. Such Internet pioneers imagined that human nature itself would change under the pressures of the new technology. They bristled at any hint that as the Internet develops, it could become more like the rest of the mundane world. But so it has. The existence of potential controls does not mean any more than the existence of potential freedom. How, for example, could authors and composers and journalists and artists survive if all their forms of information really wanted to be free? It isn't information that wants to be free; it is access to information that people want to be free. But how can it when so much labor is required to compile and interpret that information? Why shouldn't this aspect of human need—and social law—be acknowledged? Is it simply because it is not utopian? The truth is that access to recordings, books, and movies will grow with the expansion of digital entertainment networks. And in response, the publishing and recording industries will have to drastically recast themselves during the next decade, to preserve privacy and security as well as to stimulate commerce.

In the Internet counterculture the utopian fear of commerce and private property is not a spur to innovation but a harness, preventing invention. But it is not necessary to imagine that everything will be controlled any more than it is possible to envision that nothing will be. The existence of security guards does not imply a police state. The impossibility of utopian freedom does not mean the imposition of dystopian restrictions. The real is always less elegant and more complex than the ideal.

This may indeed be the most difficult conclusion. There are reasons why utopias are distant and unreachable; they can never measure up to the complexity, contradiction, and mess of the unvarnished mundane. What real world could possibly compete with a social architect's fantasy? Yet what architect's fantasy can do full justice to the unpredictability of the mundane? It may be that the best we can hope for when it comes to utopias is that they be held at arm's length and regarded as aesthetic constructions, in which various proportions are neatly worked out, contradictions eliminated, and outside intrusions minimized. They are fictions, artifacts of culture. And we should be wary if they ever become much more. There are times, in fact, when it seems as if one of the functions of culture is to dream such utopian images, to provide an imagined utopian experience without all its dangers, the wisdom without the mess of experience. What else is More's vision of no-place all about?

The word *culture*, in fact, derives from the same root as the word *cult*, with its associations of religious beliefs about agricultural cultivation. Early cults required the measurement of fields, rituals for planting, and devotional sacrifices to local deities. Participants in a farming or fertility cult had one focus: the future of the seed. Culture, in part, was an extension of cult. The word once had similar intimations of worship and reverence, along with associations with growth, propagation, and, again, cultivation. Culture has also come to mean something broader. It is a kind of social education and training, a cultivating of human possibility. It is something passed through generations, expanding the terrain of cultivation. It can also mean the entire complex of ideas and behaviors that give shape to the inchoate world, creating manners and mores and social relations. This gives culture itself a utopian impulse, since culture develops with an ideal of how society might be organized, how the next generation might behave, what deserves replacing, and what deserves renewal. Culture, in all of its meanings, is associated with devotion and development. It is a form of aspiration. It is also the realm in which aspirations are expressed and tested. American popular culture is generally better at providing pleasure than meaning; it is less interested in cultivation than comfort. But there can still be found, in the midst of contemporary cultural life, experiences that provide glimpses of utopianism and its discontents.

But no other form of expression has been so associated with the utopian dream as music. Music does not, of course, outline utopias such as those of More and Marx; particular sets of social relations are not expressed; there is no literal discussion of money or education or the moral life. But as such philosophers as Theodor Adorno have shown, music creates an autonomous world of sound with its own set of laws and relationships, its own sort of order, its own conceptions of tension and release. And in the midst of these abstract orders are encoded visions of utopia and dystopia. For now, these ideas must remain admittedly vague and suggestive and general, but my proposal is no mere speculation. Even heaven and hell have been abstractly represented in sound—and not just in programmatic plots or allusive titles. In the fifteenth century, for example, a particular musical interval, the tritone, was called "diabolus in musica"—the devil in music. Evoking the divine also involved elaborate restrictions and rules governing how music lines may contrapuntally intertwine. Explorations of the tensions between the demonic and the divine preoccupy many composers of the Western tradition, sometimes explicitly, other times metaphorically: On the one hand is dissonance and disruption, on the other harmony and resolution.

Visions of utopia, that is, are coded within the music itself. They are sometimes knit into a composer's very style. Beethoven's music, for example, with its intense concentration and controlled exclamations, is music that seems to reflect an impassioned, troubled individual finding his way in an intricate social world, in which very little is predictable or controlled. Present experience is understood by mastering what has passed. Beethoven creates a theme and then dissects it, repeats it and transforms it, almost compulsively reworking it, until all its tensions and ambiguities are brought to the surface. Only then, once a theme is mastered, can there be any sense of unfolding possibility; only then do compulsions give way to contemplation of a future, with all tensions resolved. Such temporal dramas also vary from composer to composer. Mahler, for example, unlike Beethoven, does not ruthlessly analyze the past, testing it and dissecting it. He broods about it nostalgically, recollecting it while pressing onward, ecstatically or despairingly, into the unmapped future. His music includes hints of what sorts of feelings and ideas might exist in a world in which all such tensions are resolved; his symphonies often end in utopian visions.

There are also forms of music that may almost literally take on the task of testing utopian ideas, juxtaposing desire with reality, the ideal with the real. The anthropologist Claude Lévi-Strauss, for example, once suggested that much of the familiar classical repertoire has a mythological function in modern society. After the sixteenth century, he points out, myth receded in importance; the novel and music took its place. "The music that took over the traditional function of mythology," he argues, "reached its full development with Mozart, Beethoven, and Wagner in the eighteenth and nineteenth centuries." One function of myth, in Lévi-Strauss's view, is to show how a culture's customs of marriage, government, or economy are related to more universal natural forces. It is to ground a society in nature, to disclose its divine status and prophecy possibilities. The other function is to remind a society of its boundaries: how far it can go in satisfying its desires. Myth looks forward as well as backward, to possibility as well as to limitation. It speaks about desires and limits, violations and retributions, traumatic births and ominous deaths. But these are also the themes of this music—which still lies at the heart of the Western classical repertoire. How, it asks, did we come to be? What are the forces with which we contend? What sorts of resolutions are possible? Who are our gods and who are our gods and who are our devils? What is our culture's relationship to nature? In opera, this function of myth is apparent, and not just in Wagner's overtly mythic "Ring" cycle. Again and again, opera shows the social order both animated and threatened by primal passions, and the compromises and sacrifices demanded in order to build a society. The birth of the modern state out of such conflicts was one of Verdi's great mythic themes. Similar concerns with irrational forces lying behind a rational order can be heard throughout the symphonic music of the nineteenth century, which is why the image of the devil is so prevalent in its programs. Even the virtuoso is a figure with frightening powers who seems to embody both the promise and risk of untrammeled messianism in sound. Musical myths speak with authority about our society, its fragility, its strengths, its desires, and its limits. Music becomes a wise version of the utopian messenger, pleasing us with his account of an ideal land but also warning us, in his tones, of all the dangers.

Of course, if music were unambiguously utopian, it would become almost unlistenable pap, a fantasy without boundaries or tensions. So musical paradise always comes at a price or after a horrific struggle; the greatest examples of musical utopianism, from Bach to Mahler, are tinged with the tragic. But in music, no matter what the price, there is always some vision of the future, some sense of its future failures or future promises. Unlike the visual arts, music unfolds in time; unlike theater or film, its entire structure is based upon expectations, tensions, and resolutions; unlike literature, it is never bound by literalness, it never needs testing against life as it is lived. It is realistic in the way it touches and dramatizes but it is idealistic in how it reaches far and deep.

Moreover, these dramas are not blandly recited or detachedly examined. In sound, the quest becomes lived experience; in the midst of listening we are brought into that experience. Music is ritualistic in its performance; its dramas create communities of listeners bound in similar experiences of sonic order; it creates societies, it doesn't just mirror them. And at each moment there is a question about how things will turn out or why they are turning out the way they are. At each moment we make sense of what has come before partly by imagining what is to follow; at each moment there is an imagined future. And at each moment, too, there are alternate possibilities, some shunned, others chosen. Expectations are created or disappointed or fulfilled. Desire unfolds in sound.

It may also be that if we examine the ceremonies that have developed around Western music—in particular the familiar orchestral concert—we would find ways in which utopian thought is brought out into the open, tested in real time in a real community for whom the problems of desire and dissatisfaction are never purely abstract. Consider, for example, the archetypal contours of the orthodox orchestral concert. It begins with a showy overture, proceeds to a nineteenth-century concerto with a renowned soloist, and following a twenty-minute intermission, concludes with a "serious" nine-teenth-century symphony. This musical progression suggests a movement from unrestrained and playful ego in the overture to confrontation and dialogue—the hallmarks of the concerto—concluding in the creation of a social enterprise in which individual musical voices are bound in a grand, highly ordered community. Meanwhile, the music itself—the great symphonic works of bourgeois composers ranging from Beethoven to Mahler—bears a mysterious relationship to the development of modern society. It is mythic in Lévi-Strauss's sense. The music made for the concert hall is music that tells, in effect, how concert halls came to be. The program suggests the creation of a community, from unrestrained ego through confrontation and dialogue to serious social enterprise. The concert ritual, then, is a reenactment of what may be a perennial subject of Romantic music: how the individual, like the concertgoer, may, through introspection and dream and reflection, emerge transformed as part of a new social order. The music does not promise a utopian order; it is not free of conflict; it contains its own forms of dissent and discord, its own testings of the law, its own limitations on freedom. It is utopian only in the ways it seems to bind opposing forces into a single society that seems to lie outside of time and history.

And when the music ends and the forces of the mundane again impose themselves, the silence marks the end of the dream, leaving behind a taste of what might have been if it only could be, and what exists despite our wish for what could be. We know how visions are formed and how they are shattered, how change might occur and what dangers lie in its realization, how perfection must be sought but never realized. And how, far off and far away, in some unreachable land from which only unreliable tales are told, things might be different, but that here and now, what we dream of will always lie beyond our reach. In our best of all possible worlds, that is as it should be.

SERVICE NOT INCLUDED

Herbert Muschamp

LOOS

I AM GOING TO ASSUME FOR THE PURPOSE OF THIS ESSAY THAT A UTOPIA IS a symbol of wholeness. It is a Western version of the mandala, which appears in Eastern belief systems or worldviews. It is a form of inclusion or integration that attempts to overcome or cure the ills of the differentiation necessary to civilized life. And therefore a utopian system is often distinguishable from a fascist or totalitarian one only on the basis that the utopia has not been realized.

I will also assume that idealism and amelioration of all sorts are accompanied by the same risk. Which does not mean we should not practice them, only that we should be aware of the risk. In fact, utopianism, for me, has come to represent the concept of taking local, idealistic actions in an imperfect universe. I can't think about this subject in any other way. The conventional utopia—the imaginary ideal city or world—seems to me a transitional state between belief in an almighty dignity, a supreme being capable of bending the laws of nature, and the acceptance of personal responsibility in whatever sphere life happens to place us.

I will begin by talking about one architect in particular who practiced architecture in this way. I am referring to the Viennese architect Adolf Loos. After that, I am going to talk about Surrealism and Japanese Buddhism, two systems of value that have influenced my interpretations of architecture in the contemporary city. These topics have one theme in common: the ideal of bringing subjective perception and objective reality into a relationship that is at once binary and unified.

I was in Vienna over the holidays, and while there had the opportunity to remind myself that Adolf Loos is the twentieth-century architect I most admire. Why? In the first place, he simply appeals to my taste. There's quite a lot of architecture that I respect, admire, and even love that is not at all to my personal taste, but if had the money and Loos were alive, I would hire him to design my dwelling. I like his combination of simple geometric forms and luxurious materials, and his reluctance to control residential interiors, even though many clients asked him to furnish these spaces. Critics are supposed to keep their personal taste to one side, but on this occasion I thought I'd let it out.

Loos had a passion about British tailoring, which I think was completely right for his time, in the way that Chanel was right for hers. On Christmas eve I had the pleasure of shopping for presents at Knize, the shop Loos designed. The shop is still completely intact, the clothes are still well made, the salespeople are friendly—in short, being there comes very close to my idea of a utopian experience.

Which is simply to say that Loos was a philosopher of everyday life. It would be perfectly fine to admire the architecture even if Loos didn't have a philosophy. But I suspect that if Loos didn't have a philosophy, he might never have developed the architecture he did.

What we know for certain is that for Loos, theory and practice developed hand in hand.

This in itself is an important clue to Loos's importance. He did not break theory and practice into a binary opposition. For him, rather, architecture was a form of transcending binary thinking in a way that neither practice nor theory by itself could permit. And this is just one of several dualisms that Loos reckoned with in his work. This ambition pointed Loos toward a utopian idea of wholeness.

His synthesis of unadorned forms and luxurious materials is another example of this. So is his articulation of the difference between interior and exterior space. The exterior, Loos believed, should be socially exemplary. It should be Spartan; it should not try to impress people, stand out, arouse envy, or call attention to wealth. Spartan Loos's exteriors certainly were, but they certainly do stand out, and like other examples of understated taste, they have the power to make others feel inferior; they imply a form of moral, esthetic, and social judgment that caused considerable discomfort to the Viennese of Loos's day.

It's true that Viennese artists in Loos's day could be intellectual bullies and cultural snobs, that they were always at risk of flying too high above the heads of humanity. This is something the Viennese themselves argued about constantly. It is the theme of the Hofmannstahl-Strauss opera *The Woman Without a Shadow*. The woman is the daughter of a god, a stand-in for the creature of remote, esthetic regions. In order to become a person and thereby gain a shadow, she must renounce her supernatural powers and perform an act of human kindness for a woman of humble station. This was Hofmannstahl's allegorical representation of his own struggle to recognize that art alone could not perform tasks of reform that called for social and political action.

Loos recognized this as well. Or, I should say, for him aesthetic and social values were fundamentally as indivisible as theory and practice. In addition to his private houses, Loos built many units of social housing in Vienna in the period after the Great War. In fact, he served on the city's housing commission. But Loos did not equate aesthetic values exclusively with his private commissions, nor social values with his public ones. He resigned from the housing group, for example, when it rejected one of his plans on aesthetic grounds.

Iris Murdoch says that the pivot between our inner and outer worlds is a fundamental point of moral action. We can all have fantasies about blowing up the world or remaking it in our image, and these are usually signs that we've lost touch with our own humanity and lost respect for the humanity of others. Loos's articulation of the difference between interior and exterior is thus a form of social service. It's a recognition that entering and leaving a building should be a point of considered transition.

He did not believe, as many modern architects after him insisted, that interiors and exteriors should be designed in a uniform vocabulary. He did not seek to abolish the distinction between them. He did not try to dematerialize walls into transparent membranes. He wanted architecture to mark the passage between the two related spheres of subjective perception and objective reality, while the building as a whole represented the possibility of a unity between them. It was a gestalt, in other words, a whole that is more than the sum of its parts.

Loos's most famous building, designed for another men's tailor on Michaelerplatz, was called the "House Without Eyebrows," because its windows lacked cornices and other decorative trim. Legendarily, the emperor pulled the curtains in his apartment, which directly faced it, so that he wouldn't have to look at it.

If the story is true, or even if it's only apocryphal, those curtains should be considered one of Loos's major achievements. In effect, they completed his building. Under the Habsburgs, or any other absolute monarchy for that matter, objective reality was an extension of subjective perception. The palace windows had always shown an outside world that conformed to imperial will. The Loos building signified that this was no longer the case.

Although Loos was compelled to add flower boxes to the windows, and they are actually quite sweet, his aesthetic was an antithesis of Biedermeier taste. More important, the Loos building had the gall to be something other than an object. Loos's windows had the temerity to look back—to stare at the Hofburg—as wide as their sockets would allow. The emperor was not willing to contemplate a reality over which he no longer exercised control. He was compelled to declare, by pulling some fabric over the glass, that subjectivity and objectivity were not one and the same. He was compelled, against his will, to become a critic. In so doing he became a citizen, and performed the citizen's role of revealing the conflicts architecture provokes.

Loos has been called a functionalist. But he did not regard machines as objects of beauty, and he did not think that buildings were works of art. He insisted that the meaning and value of a pipe concern what it does, not what it looks like. He argued for making a clear distinction between utilitarian urns and aesthetically articulated vases. To appreciate his emphasis on this distinction it is helpful to recall that he was a close friend and intellectual soul mate of Ludwig Wittgenstein.

Wittgenstein believed that modern philosophy was little more than the working out of word games that did not refer to reality as such but betrayed an imprisonment within a framework of concepts developed by classical philosophy. The way out of the prison was to recognize the rhetoric. Once you did that, the framework would drop away, like the vines around Sleeping Beauty's castle. The point of philosophical work, then, was to expose the limits imposed by language and thereby correct perceptual distortions.

Loos's architecture had a similar ambition. To strip away ornament was to strip away rhetoric. The goal was the critical one of clarity, or, if you like, the philosophical one of the Good. It was Wittgenstein, in fact, who took this idea to its most extreme architectural expression in the house he co-designed with Paul Englemann for his sister Gretl in Kundmanngasse, Vienna. The windows become even more pronounced—the entire exterior is composed around the windows, while even the doors are made of metal-framed glass. Materials were chosen strictly on the basis of durability.

But we must keep in mind that metal, stone, and particularly glass require a continual ritual of cleaning and that, in a house by Wittgenstein, cleaning has an almost ritualistic meaning. The vision of the Good is a place where vision is good. Glass is clear, and perception should also be unclouded by the distortions that language imposes upon it. One cannot just install glass in a frame and let it sit there. Dust and fog must also be polished from perceptions.

As I've indicated, Loos's ideas and projects invited criticism all along the way, in his time and in ours. These must be appreciated as extensions of the polishing process undertaken by his buildings. The buildings coax opinions, positive and negative, into revealing themselves. The result is a conflict between the desire to expose and the even stronger desire to overlook.

I believe that the production of this kind of conflict is the most important cultural function that great cities perform. I arrived at this concept simply by turning around an idea of D. W. Winnicott, the British psychoanalyst. Winnicott once said that artists are people driven by the conflict between a desire to communicate and an even stronger desire to hide. The conflict between the desire to expose and the desire to overlook seems to me (and perhaps many others who work in daily journalism) to be the dynamic that drives a great city forward. When people think of utopias they ordinarily think not in terms of conflict but in terms of harmony. But it could be that the translation of conflict into the cultural sphere is a step toward the realization of peace.

Loos viewed his mission as utopian, but in a somewhat ironic spirit. In 1908 he wrote, "I made the following discovery and offered it to the world: cultural evolution is synonymous with the disappearance of ornament from utensils. I thought I was bringing new joy to the world, which did not thank me. People were gloomy and hung their heads. What depressed one man was the realization that no new ornament can be created. Then I said, Don't shed any tears. See, that's what makes for greatness in our time: that it is incapable of producing ornament, we have finally made our way to the absence of ornamentation. Look, the day is at hand, our fulfillment is waiting, Soon the city streets will gleam like white walls. Like Zion, the holy city, the capital of heaven. Then we will be fulfilled."

SURREALISM

In 1926 Loos designed a house in Montmartre for the Dada-Surrealist poet Tristan Tzara, and the only reason I mention this is to make a little segue to the next thing I want to talk about: the use of Surrealism as an analytic device.

For there is another way to deal with the distortions caused by rhetoric, which is to exaggerate them to the point that people recognize that their minds are being manipulated. This was the technique used by the Wachowski brothers in *The Matrix*, which I consider the great urban architectural allegory of our time. Now and then there will be a little glitch in the transmission of the matrix environment, like a fast-reverse déjà vu or a ripple in the curtain wall of a glass skyscraper, which clues us to the fact that the matrix world around us is an electronically manufactured illusion being fed into our skulls.

I use similar effects in writing about architecture, because I think that architecture is also a medium of mental conditioning as well as a form of art or social practice. I like to sketch an image of a building or a cityscape and then create the impression that some corner of the object is twisting or bending, flattening from three dimensions into two, or stretching out in the dimension of time. I do this to remind readers that what they're reckoning with is mental pictures, signs in their interior landscapes, not merely physical objects in space. I do try very hard to make the mental images correspond accurately to material objects in space, using description, metaphor, and analysis, but it's important to call attention to the difference between objects and mental images occasionally simply because that distinction is an important aspect of reality. The cleanest glass imaginable, in other words, can in itself be a distortion if we think that the picture it frames corresponds to an objective truth.

I call myself a Surrealist. This sometimes puzzles people. After all, the Surrealist movement in art is supposed to have petered out by the end of the 1940s, but I was born in 1947. Maybe I just absorbed it from the atmosphere. But the main reason I call myself a Surrealist is that criticism tends to be ideologically based, even or perhaps especially when critics themselves are unaware of it. As it has come down to us, architecture criticism is typically a composite of eighteenth-century academic theory crossed with liberal social reform, nineteenth-century historicism, Romantic impressionism, and twentieth-century formalism. In various forms, it repeats the debates between Ancients and Moderns, or advocates of Classical or Gothic style.

For me, Surrealism is above all a dual mode of analysis that attempts to deal with the relationship between our inner and outer worlds. The two poles of Surrealist thought are Marx and Freud, and these are also for me two ways to describe events. I'm not referring to classical Marx and Freud but to the schools of thought they initiated: two ways of structuring history, social history and personal history, through an examination of conflicts. Both schools of thought are based on an analogy with the medical model of diagnosis and cure. The Surrealist attempt to fuse them displays the utopian attraction to wholeness, and as a practical matter of application it is to be more feared than welcomed.

But the diagnostic component is still useful—more useful, I think, than anything that has come along since. We have a habit of wanting to discard value systems in favor of new ones. Sometimes this is healthy, sometimes not. But a good way to buck the system is to retrieve a way of thought that's been unfairly tainted with the charge of obsolescence.

I doubt that Marx and Freud can be unified in a single analytic system. However, Surrealism defined these two systems as brackets within which the world of forms operates. Art is a way of mediating between them, on an ongoing, historically grounded basis.

There is a historical line of creative responses to this space. For example, if you visit Vienna today, you are seeing the remains of a city whose cultural and intellectual life was substantially driven by these responses. Freud didn't come out of nowhere, nor did the architectural achievements of the Red Vienna period after World War I, in particular the monumental Karl Marx housing project. Gustave Klimt, Karl Kraus, Hans Hofmann, Loos, Hugo von Hofmannstahl, and Arthur Schnitzler were engaged with the tensions between the realm of politics and the realm of psychology, or between social and aesthetic reform. That is why Vienna is often regarded as the birthplace of modernism. The intersection of public and private space is what the Viennese coffeehouse signified.

And that is also what modernism signifies to me. It is more a matter of ideas than it is of forms. Some architects, such as Ludwig Mies van der Rohe, pursued it with expressed structure and, particularly, the use of glass to reduce the building skin to a transparent membrane. Others, such as Frank Lloyd Wright, developed it with the open floor plan and the corner window. Or, like Theo van Doesburg, they pursued it with primary colors, flat planes, and moveable partitions.

Aldo Rossi developed the idea further by merging personal and collective memories of the classical tradition, in the manner of De Chirico. Frank Gehry is developing it today with a combination of industrial materials, curvilinear forms, and voluptuous, free-form interiors. Rem Koolhaas does it by synthesizing (rational) grids with (emotive) spirals, by fusing the rigor of Mies with the theatricality of Wallace Harrison, by casting classical Euclidean shapes in vulgar materials. Jean Nouvel and Philippe Starck do it by eroticizing industrially manufactured forms.

These projects parallel works by Virginia Woolf, James Joyce, Igor Stravinsky, Pablo Picasso, Federico Fellini, Alfred Hitchcock, George Balanchine, Maxime Gorky, Christopher Isherwood, Robert Rauschenberg, and other artists who have sought to capture the interplay between perception and reality in the immediate, heightened form with which it is actually experienced in urban life.

I think that it is often more difficult to appreciate this form in the individual work of art. That is partly because we may not be conscious of its relationship to other artworks on which much of its meaning and value may depend. This is particularly true in the United States, where things tend to exist in a vacuum. This atomization is nothing new. When the country was very young, Tocqueville wrote about the huge void separating individual citizens from common concerns. And he predicted the Surrealist form that our culture would eventually take: "I do not fear that the poetry of democratic nations will prove insipid or that it will fly too near the ground. I rather apprehend that it will be forever losing itself in the clouds and that it will range at last to purely imaginary regions, that the fantastic beings of democratic poets may sometimes make us regret the world of reality."

We can see this prediction borne out in two architectural forms. One is the architecture of distraction—in theme parks, shopping malls, gambling resorts, neotraditional towns, and other highly controlled pseudourban environments. These are inadvertently Surreal, even when they are trying to be Surreal. They are symptoms rather than creative responses.

The second is in projects that knowingly project subjective perception into the public realm. This is the ultimate significance of

Frank Gehry's design for the Bilbao Guggenheim work. He uses a vocabulary derived from fine art, that is, one that comes in under the sign of subjective expression, to displace or challenge the idea that architecture should be driven by obedience to an external authority, such as reason, history, the machine, and so on.

It's possible for architecture to be merely symptomatic, or to ignore the issue of psychology altogether. But in my judgment the most interesting work being done today is exploring the issues of boundaries, borders, bridges, transitional spaces, and urban relationships. If this work is cutting-edge or avant-garde, it also belongs to a very long history of ideas. Surrealism simply offers an inherently unstable interpretive method for interpreting new work in a historical context.

BUDDHISM

Wittgenstein may be best known for this statement: "Whatever can be said can be said clearly, and that of which one cannot speak, one must be silent about."

Religion, like talent, is something of which one is not supposed to speak, certainly not in a secular context such as art, architecture, or urbanism. And in fact I don't think that it's possible to speak about the essential qualities of religious experience. In any case, this is something I don't propose to try, in part because one of the reasons I practice religion is to hold in check my natural inclination to turn everything into a story.

However, when I accepted the invitation to discuss the theme of utopia, I knew that I couldn't avoid talking about my religious practice, because I'd be avoiding the most interesting story I have to tell on that subject.

I practice a form of Buddhism established by a school that was founded in the thirteenth-century. Like other Buddhist schools, it does propose the existence of a supreme being. It is, however, based on faith, and it is accompanied by a large body of elegant theory about life. The theories I think one can talk about. Whether or not you're a practitioner, the theories bring considerable clarity to the issue of utopia. My criticism is sometimes criticized for being antitheory. It's true that I've always been skeptical about theories developed in 1970s Paris. The theories I rely on were substantially developed by the Tien T'ai school of Buddhism in ninth-century China and were later embraced by schools in medieval Japan.

Like other schools of Mahayana Buddhism, mine is based on the Lotus Sutra, in which it is stated that even the lowest life forms possess the state of Buddhahood within their present life condition. We don't have to go through countless rebirths and practice austerities to reach this state. The point of practice is to center one's life around it. Lotuses grow in swamps. If you put them in a fabulous blue David Hockney swimming pool, they would die. They need the muck of a swamp to grow and turn into beautiful flowers. From the lotus symbol it is to be inferred that the world will always be, in effect, a swamp. There is always going to be a lot of mud around. The challenge is to turn the mud into food for one's enlightenment.

Therefore it is theoretically useless, and potentially even destructive, to imagine a stable world of perfect bliss, harmony, or even efficiency. It's just not going to happen. Efforts to make it happen are likely to create a dystopian state. This is not to say that people should resign themselves to living like swamp creatures. It is to say that enlightenment and the swamp are not indivisible spheres of existence. The swamp is a given. One must actively make the cause for enlightenment.

Another property of the lotus is that it flowers and seeds at the same time. In Buddhist theory, this symbolizes the simultaneity of cause and effect. If you make a cause—by thought, word, or action —you are producing its effect at the same time. You may not experience the effect until later, but one of the goals of Buddhist practice is to see that this delay is a property of the world we live in. If you make the cause of enlightenment, you are actually entering an enlightened state, which simply means that you are less likely over time to keep bumping into the same furniture.

Japanese Buddhism organizes experience into ten worlds or life conditions, ranging from hell to enlightenment. These are hierarchically organized into six lower worlds and four higher worlds. The highest of the six lower worlds is called heaven, or rapture. It corresponds to many of the utopian schemes we have seen, and also much of the advertising we see on television. Club Med is pitched at this level. So, for me, is shopping at the Knize store on the night before Christmas. Others might find it in a midnight choral service on the same evening. For many, architecture should ideally aim for this level. When people look at photographs of, say, Luis Barragan's landscapes, they might think that this is perfect and that everyone should live this way.

But the important thing to keep in mind is that, blissful though it may be, it is still one of the lower worlds. Happiness, however, or the Good, can only be found in the four higher worlds. The difference between higher and lower worlds is that the lower ones are all reactive. They are passive responses to environmental stimuli. The reason why Club Med is blissful is because it offers temporary relief from the environment of everyday life. We attain the higher worlds, by contrast, by engaging actively with the environment of everyday life. I'm only interested in the concept of utopian architecture and urbanism as it applies to this form of engagement.

The words for these worlds are learning, realization, *bodhisattva*, and Buddhahood. The New York Public Library is a temple to the world of learning. On a good day I spend time in that world, too. The ticket to this world is admitting that you don't have the answers. It's a world where humility feels good; it has nothing to do with low self-esteem. On the contrary, it's a great relief to know that other people before you have faced confusing circumstances similar to your own and managed to make sense of them. I was in my mid-twenties before I learned how to learn, and now I have a passion for it. I think of the architects I write about as my teachers. As in any school, there are good and bad ones. I think of the readers, too, as teachers, and sometimes as fellow students. But I'm particularly interested in the architects, past and present, who have something valuable to teach about contemporary urban life—which means that they offer creative responses to the relationship between our inner and outer worlds.

This relationship corresponds to a Buddhist concept called *kyochi myogyo*. *Kyo* and *chi* respectively refer to subjective perception and objective reality. *Myogyo* is a term that refers to the concept of "two but not two"—two things that are distinct but not separable. For instance, the face and obverse of a coin are two but not two. Each of them is distinct, but one supposes the existence of the other. You can aim to create a utopia, but you must be aware that there will always be a dystopian side to it, and that this side can dominate.

This is the message of *The Matrix*, and in part of H. G. Wells's *The Time Machine* also. Society creates these machines to do its dirty work and then the machines turn human beings into their batteries. The goal of the heroes is to awaken others to the reality of the dystopia they actually live in.

What I look for in a building is what environmentalists call an "eco-tone," the overlapping area between two adjacent ecosystems that is an ecosystem in itself. That is why I see buildings simply as pieces of the city. When I was hired at the *New York Times*, the editors said they hoped I wouldn't write about buildings as if they were free-floating objects in space. They wanted more of the con-nective tissue. All I've really done at the paper is follow their guid-ance in two directions, which I've already talked about: deeper into mental conflicts, farther out into economic and social conflicts.

It was not possible, for example, to write about the 1999 redesign of City Hall Park without going in these directions. You couldn't sim-ply talk about the aesthetics. To the eye, the park presented a fairly innocuous period rendition of the nineteenth-century picturesque park, completely with marble fountain, gas lamps, cast-iron fences, and other simulated Frederick Law Olmsted effects. But, as we know, these trappings were merely the ornament for an ambitious securi-ty designed to further insulate City Hall from the people of New York. The park was parsley, in other words, and who wants to read about parsley? But if you see the park and the security system as two adja-cent ecosystems, then you have an ecotone with its own properties, such as paranoid-schizoid urbanism, that are worth analyzing. As Iris Murdoch might have said, the ecotone is a pivot between public and private space and therefore a place for moral action. Or, as in the case of City Hall, an amoral act of self-deception.

Realization is where a lot of the best teachers hang out. This is a world where people begin to learn directly from their own experi-ences, as well as from the examples of others. Realization is the world of creative responses, fresh ideas, new interpretations, innovative ways of saying things that haven't been said before in quite the same way. Those in this world tend to challenge existing dogmas, social and aesthetic restraints, perceptions that no longer correspond to cultural realities. This is the world of artists, even of architects such as Loos, who deny that they are artists.

People in the worlds of learning and realization tend to be self-centered, however. They are more concerned with their own fulfillment than with that of others. They are definitely above the lower worlds of reaction but are not fully enlightened to the fact that their own fulfillment is contingent on that of others. They think life is about them. They have yet to understand the idea of service.

The ninth world is the world of the bodhisattva. This is where the idea of service kicks in. We've all seen those great statues of bodhisattva, and we recognize them because they all wear the same bodhisattva smile. And the reason why they are smiling is they've discovered that the joy of serving others overrides the suffering we all encounter in the world of the swamp. A bodhisattva is a person who has renounced or postponed his or her enlightenment until others are on the road to theirs.

I think it is possible to undertake architecture as a bodhisattva practice. For example, advocates of green architecture or sustainable design probably make up the largest cluster of architects working in this sphere today. Their mission is the closest we have to a utopian enterprise. They are engaged with reforming the furthest extremities of our inner and outer worlds—with perception and objective reality—and their work helps to define the richness of the cultural ecotone between them.

Architects who dedicate themselves to social housing, public transportation, public space, and historic preservation are also conducting architecture as a bodhisattva practice. They may not enjoy the celebrity attained by others in their profession. But they create, maintain, and reinforce the connective tissue on which the life of the city depends. They have more respect than others for the dignity of life.

I also think it is possible to conduct the more exalted form of architecture—buildings conceived with the ambition of aesthetic appeal—as a bodhisattva practice. Art is a form of connective tissue. This is what the concept of poetry meant to the Greeks. For them a poem was not just a euphonic arrangement of words. It was the product of a medium through which values, memories, beliefs, emotions, conflicts, and perceptions were circulated throughout culture. Buildings, similarly, are not discrete objects. They are building blocks of a democratic society. W. H. Auden once proposed that a civilization could be judged by "the degree of diversity attained and the degree of unity attained." In the spirit of service, architecture can contribute to both. Without the spirit of service, architecture can be a highly destructive force.

The tenth and top world is Buddhahood. The only thing I can say about this condition is that everyone is supposed to have it. In theory, it is ahistorical, but in this world it finds expression in the historical circumstances in which bodhisattva practice is carried out.

I want to end with a few words about how architectural criticism fits into the utopian prospect. In Buddhism there is a concept called *shaku-buku*, which literally means "crush and destroy." It sounds wonderfully violent. But it actually refers to the practice of correcting distorted views, whether one's own or other people's. And this I think, is what a critic does. My own writing is more interpretive than evaluative, because I want to highlight the values, good or bad, that buildings embody. And this often involves challenging common assumptions and exposing their limitations, even those made by admirable figures.

For example, Buckminster Fuller was a genius and a great utopian, but he used to go around saying, "Reform the environment, not man," which seems to me an erroneous view. I can understand why he said it; he wanted to ward off the risk of totalitarian mind control. But the truth is that men's and women's minds are being reformed constantly, these days mostly by television, whether we like it or not, and it's the responsibility of culture to make accessible the means by which people can gain traction against these environmental pressures.

Or, to cite a more recent example, many architects involved with the Congress for the New Urbanism are very idealistic, and there is much to admire in the solidarity achieved by this movement. But I don't think that they have earned the title "urban", since to me "urban" means a belief that the lotus needs the swamp, and vice versa. It's not a good idea to encourage those who want to flee from the complexities of urban life.

Words are the instrument I have at my disposal, and this is fine, because I agree with Wittgenstein that language lies at the root of many problems. The misuse of the word *urban* is one example. You don't have to be a Buddhist to realize the extent to which our culture is plagued by dualistic ways of thinking that distort our view of reality. The polarization of architecture into "modern" and "traditional" continues to obstruct the city from reckoning with contemporary social issues, like the increasing commercialization and privatization of public space. The severing of aesthetics from ethics has produced other distortions. So has the tendency to polarize people artificially into pro- or anti- factions on issues raised by real estate development, architectural preservation, or theory, when what we should really be talking about are the manifold realities of life in the capitals of advanced capitalism in the post–Cold War era.

I think that writers are unusually conscious of these dualistic practices because we're always falling into them—on one hand, on the other hand, et cetera. They are useful rhetorical devices. But I'm always practicing *shaku-buku* on myself to deal with rhetoric problems. In doing this, I try to serve readers. Readers have the opportunity to decide for themselves where and how to create an ecotone, a border between their inner and outer words. My goal is to produce a useful vocabulary for readers who want to take this opportunity.

"BUT EVEN SO, LOOK AT THAT":
AN IRONIC PERSPECTIVE ON UTOPIAS

Martin E. Marty

"WHY DEVOTE SEASONS OF YOUR LIFE TO THE STUDY OF UTOPIAS? YOU DO know, don't you, that every one ever proposed or realized has failed." So a friend set out to divert me from a prolonged inquiry into utopianism. Yes, I know of utopian failures. Yet the world would be poorer had no one ever dreamed dreams of the no-place (u-topia) that is home to "perfect" sets of human arrangements. One looks for a way to rescue something positive from utopian experiments, since they can also inspire world-weariness and cynicism in the mode of those who groan: "Everything has been tried. Nothing works."

One way to approach human error is to see it as a stimulus to the imagination. The late Lewis Thomas, a medical doctor who headed the Memorial Sloan-Kettering Cancer Center in New York, has helped shape my views on this. Particularly provocative has been his short essay "To Err Is Human," in *The Medusa and the Snail: More Notes of a Biology Watcher*. Thomas there addresses accidental errors. He observes that "mistakes are at the very base of human thought, embedded there, feeding the structure like root nodules." In the face of actions that reveal them, we look on and learn to say that we learn by "trial and error." Thomas notes that we don't say we learn by "trial and rightness" or by "trial and triumph."

Take that issue of error, urged the good doctor. When we ascribe learning not to triumph but to such error, we observe that "the old phrase puts it that way because that is, in real life, the way it is done." Thus, says Thomas of any particular occasion marked by error, "if it is a lucky day, and a lucky laboratory, somebody makes a mistake: the wrong buffer, something in one of the blanks, a decimal mis-placed in reading counts, the warm room off by a degree and a half," and so forth. Whatever the mistake, "when the results come in, something is obviously screwed up, and then the action can begin."

Here is the decisive point for Thomas and, I would like to show, for those who pick up the pieces after utopias break or after the bulk of original plans for them head for the wastebasket: "The misreading is not the important error; it opens the way. The next step is the crucial one. If the investigator can bring himself to say, 'But even so, look at that!' then the new finding, whatever it is, is ready for snatching. What is needed, for progress to be made, is the move based on the error."

"But even so, look at that!" One therewith hears an awe-filled "Behold!" That is indeed fitting. The Greek word for "beholding" is *theoria,* the root of our English word *theory.* It is at the moment of beholding that new thinking, new theory, and fresh imagination come into play.

Of course, moral, spiritual, and intellectual errors resulting from vice, weakness, insecurity, or folly are of a somewhat different character than are the laboratory accidents to which Thomas refers. But they all can give rise to beholding, to theorizing—and to consequent action, to "snatching," as Thomas puts it. "Whenever new kinds of thinking are about to be accomplished, or new varieties of music, there has to be argument beforehand." In argument—and utopian planning is always set forth as a kind of against-the-grain argument—"the hope is in the faculty of wrongness, the tendency toward error. The capacity to leap across mountains of information to land lightly on the wrong side represents the highest of human endowments."

Thomas even applies this line of thought to futures, more or less as utopians do: "How, for instance, should we go about organizing ourselves for social living on a planetary scale, now that we have become, as a plain fact of life, a single community? We can assume, as a working hypothesis, that all the right ways of doing this are unworkable. What we need, then, for moving ahead, is a set of wrong alternatives much longer and more interesting than the short list of mistaken courses that any of us can think up right now."

DEFINING UTOPIA: SEARCHING FOR ORDER, SEEING DISORDER
Having borrowed the insight to inform inquiry about utopias, I shall also efficiently borrow a tentative definition of utopia rather than turn this whole essay into an effort at definition. In his preface to *The Obsolete Necessity: America in Utopian Writings, 1888–1900,* Kenneth M. Roemer speaks succinctly to our need: "Utopia, outopos, eutopos, dystopia, kakotopia, Utopians, utopists, utopographers—the study of imaginary ideal societies is burdened with enough strange-sounding names to convince an interloper to take a course in Greek cognates. I have tried to keep my terms as simple as possible: utopia—hypothetical [let me add: sometimes actually effected] community, society, or world reflecting a more perfect, alternative way of

life; Utopian—being (usually humans) who live in utopia; a Utopian work—a piece of literature depicting a particular utopia; a utopian author—a person who writes a Utopian work."

Behind many analyses of utopia, including mine, is the recognition that at their heart is some version of a search for order. Such a quest is, if not a human universal, then still sufficiently widespread that it can help attract audiences for utopian claims and ventures. In a provocative book, *Patterns of Order and Utopia,* Dorothy F. Donnelly, who provides a small anthology of testimonies to this conjunction, quotes Rudolf Arnhem. He claimed that human "striving for order . . . derives from a similar universal tendency throughout the organized world; it is also paralleled by, and perhaps derived from, the striving towards the state of simplest structure in physical systems." More familiar is the claim of Simone Weil: "The first of the soul's needs, the one which touches most nearly its eternal destiny, is order." Donnelly herself hinges everything on "the integral relation between the idea of order and the classical Utopia, and," she adds, "the emphasis is on the proposition that the expression of the desire for a better way of being in the classical Utopia centered, first and foremost, on redefining order."

Some reservations begin to come from Isaiah Berlin, who relates a dark "under side" of human nature to utopia, and sees also a place for disorder: "The search for perfection does seem to me a recipe for bloodshed, no better even if it is demanded by the sincerest of idealists, the purest of heart. No more rigorous moralist than Immanuel Kant has ever lived, but even he said, in a moment of illumination, 'Out of the crooked timber of humanity no straight thing was ever made.' To force people into the neat uniforms demanded by dogmatically believed-in schemes is almost always the road to inhumanity. We can only do what we can; but that we must do, against difficulties".

Berlin elsewhere explicitly applied this insight to utopias and utopianism: "Any faith in a single static pattern embracing the whole of mankind is blown to pieces. Pluralism entails that Utopia is not so much unrealisable in practical terms as inconceivable, given the nature of human values. All enterprises based on the search for a perfect society are given the lie by this devastating claim."

Berlin went on to treat utopias also as double-sided. Thus: *"Utopias have their value—nothing so wonderfully expands the imaginative horizons of human potentialities—but as guides to conduct they can prove literally fatal. Heraclitus was right, things cannot stand still"* (italics mine).

THE NEED FOR A PERSPECTIVE: HUMANE IRONY AND UTOPIA

We will here refer briefly to three classic utopias. To bring them to focus, one needs a perspective from which to interpret them. My proposal is to employ a concept proposed by Richard Reinitz, "humane irony." Nothing else so well combines the notion of irony for someone who deals with utopias, and humane concern for the agents and victims of ironic outcomes. Reinitz elaborates on a theme of midcentury American Protestant theologian Reinhold Niebuhr: "We perceive a human action as ironic . . . when we see the consequences of that action as contrary to the original intention of the actor and can locate a significant part of the reason for the discrepancy in the actor himself or in his intention." Why does Reinitz include the adjective *humane* before this form of ironic perception? "Humane irony is a form for historical perception that directs us to examine people in all their self-contradiction and the situation in which they act in all of its complexity." He continues:

"The discreet sympathy engendered by this kind of irony, involving at once an acceptance of the humanity of the historical actor and a critical stance toward the consequences of his actions allows for both the empathetic encounter with people of the past that makes historical knowledge possible and the analytic distance from them that makes it useful."

Observers who give voice to humane irony are not free to pronounce particular utopian intentions as being simply good and then account for their subsequent frustration by reference to fate or accident. At the same time, they are not given license to declare the self-same or similar utopian aspirations to be unequivocally bad, meaning foolish, malign, or exploitative, and then account for their devastation by reference to unmitigated evil in the heart and mind of utopian agents.

In this context my thesis is that those who wish to make assessments of utopias and utopian writing or experiment past and present, or to use them for projections into the future, do best to view them ironically. But they should do so employing the special version of the ironic perspective for which we have adopted the term "humane irony."

In lectures that Niebuhr delivered in 1949 and 1951 and on the first page of a book published in 1952, *The Irony of American History,* the theologian applied this perspective to the postwar United States and the Cold War Soviet Union. Niebuhr pointed to four dimensions of the ironic perspective, which are relevant for understanding utopians and their character. Here I break his paragraph apart typographically to stress how promising they are to provide a framework for analyzing the present topic. As you read them, think of utopia and utopians:

> If virtue becomes vice through some
> hidden defect in the virtue;

> if strength becomes weakness because of the vanity
> to which strength may prompt the mighty man or
> nation [or cause];
>
> if security is transmuted into insecurity because too
> much reliance is placed upon it;
>
> if wisdom becomes folly because it does not know
> its limits—
>
> in all such cases the situation is ironic.

I take the liberty of adding one more, equally relevant to the utopian impulse:

> If its drive for order results in the creation of disorder
> because there is underestimation of human limits
> and historical contingency, the same is true.

Niebuhr then more specifically contrasts the ironic to two other tropes that could inform some observers of utopia:

> The ironic situation is distinguished from a pathetic
> one by the fact that the person involved in it bears
> some responsibility for it.
>
> It is differentiated from tragedy by the fact that the
> responsibility is related to an unconscious weakness
> rather than to a conscious resolution.

Niebuhr did make explicit reference to utopianism in the context of dream-filled idealists. Their confidence, he wrote, that "the highest ends of life can be fulfilled in man's historic existence" makes for "Utopian visions of historical possibilities on the one hand and for rather materialistic conceptions of human ends on the other." As one becomes ever more familiar with concrete utopias throughout history, the confidence their fashioners and followers brought and their frustration in ironic terms become ever more obvious.

Niebuhr concluded with a chapter called "The Significance of

Irony," reference to which completes the framework preparing us for a review of utopias. It begins with a bit of helpful self-review: "Is the discernment of an ironic element . . . merely the fruit of a capricious imagination? Is the pattern of irony superimposed upon the historical data which are so various that they would be tolerant of almost any pattern, which the observer might care to impose?"

Niebuhr invoked a biblical passage to propose a transcendent background to his interpretation. After reviewing some aspects of the American endeavor, he wrote, "Over these exertions we discern by faith the ironical laughter of the divine source and end of all things. 'He that sitteth in the heavens shall laugh' (Psalm 2:4). God laughs because 'the people imagine a vain thing.'"

This is the point at which some may think we are abandoning readers who have been looking for something to redeem from utopias. Are they to be marooned with a sneering and condescending deity? No. It was precisely at this point that Niebuhr began to introduce the element that rendered his irony humane. His words contain what have to sound surprising to those who approach the concept for the first time:

> The scripture assures us that God's laughter is derisive, having the sting of judgment upon our vanities in it. But if the laughter is truly ironic it must symbolize mercy as well as judgment. For whenever judgment defines the limits of human striving it creates the possibility of an humble acceptance of those limits. Within that humility mercy and peace find a lodging place.

Niebuhr reminded readers that

> irony cannot be directly experienced. The knowledge of it depends upon an observer who is not so hostile to the victim of irony as to deny the element of virtue

> which must constitute a part of the ironic situation; nor yet so sympathetic as to discount the weakness, the vanity and pretension which constitute another element. Since the participant in an ironic situation cannot, unless he be very self-critical, fulfill this later condition, the knowledge of irony is usually reserved for observers rather than participants.

So there has to be a distinction between observers of utopia and devisers of utopianisms or the ironic victims thereof.

> If participants in an ironic situation become conscious of the vanities and illusions which make an ironic situation more than merely comic, they would tend to abate the pretensions and dissolve the irony. Purely hostile observers, on the other hand, may laugh bitterly at the comedy in an ironic situation, but they could not admit the virtue in the intentions which miscarry so comically.

Niebuhr always used the word *utopian* deprecatorily, as we need not. He employed the term to critique the mentality that expects that at some moment in history the chaos of our world can and will be overcome and that social evil will be eliminated in a state of complete harmony and fulfilled meaning. In such a case, absolute moral ideals, impossible to attain and never to be seen as transcending the zone of argument and self-examination, get attached to human society. There they cannot be realized.

THREE CLASSIC UTOPIAS

To talk meaningfully about utopianism, one must talk about utopias, whether imagined in literary works or exemplified in planned, built, and peopled communities. In doing so, it is most worthwhile for us to concentrate on several formative instances and then draw some tentative conclusions based on observations about them. Thereupon readers can test the usefulness of this perspective on communities of their own choosing. It is time to specialize.

My colleagues in this book write as critics of music and architecture. I am drawing on utopias that have impetus from and bearing on the world of religion. There was a period of great unsettlement in Europe during the breaking up of the Middle Ages and the forming of the modern, when the tradition of utopias that is still with us had its start. We shall choose three of these: Thomas More's *Utopia*, Thomas Müntzer's preached and fought-for effort to reconstitute the apostolic church and build a society around it in towns such as Allstedt, Germany; and Johann Andreae's *Christianopolis*. More's work is dated 1516; Müntzer's efforts came to a climax during the Peasants' War in 1525, when he met his death. Andreae's effort follows by almost a century, after the unsatisfying post-Reformation settlements and on the eve of the Thirty Years' War (1618–1648) and at the edges of the Enlightenment.

More's is a *humanist* utopia. A Catholic, More tells of a human city based on intellect and reason, not on divine revelation or churchly teaching. It includes a celebration of religious tolerance by a man who pursued heretics.

Müntzer did not create a utopia in his writing; he preached elements of one. His is a radical Reformation Protestant utopia, to be realized through violent revolution. The peace it promised never came.

Andreae's is an orthodox Reformation Protestant utopia. Andreae, a Lutheran, points to a "city" founded on very rigid and stipulated doctrinal and moral codes, which, it was presumed, reason confirms. Its concepts are not salable beyond the very community that elicited it.

Since it is impossible to detail these utopias and utopian times in one essay, and since we are concentrating on only one theme—that the perspective of humane irony can best inform study of them—let us quickly anticipate some of the ironic outcomes.

In the case of the first, we will connect the author's proposal with the course of conduct of his life. In *Utopia*, More depicted a community based on religious tolerance that did not insist upon Catholicism or any other form of Christianity as its definer and boundary. More assumed, in the luxury of pre-Enlightenment English times, that his utopians could represent wisdom, order, and virtue. While sure of himself, he was not arrogant or pharisaical, yet there is no doubt that he saw his own favored kind of humanism validly projected in that imagined place. Yet when the test posed by the Reformation came, humanistic tolerance failed More, or he failed to entertain it. The luxury of being tolerant disappeared. He had built no safeguards into his own personal "city" and had no way of using what he had set forth in his book to bring order to Reformation England. More quickly abandoned all guise of tolerance and struck out with fury in verbal violence that encouraged others to use violence. The folly and disorder—yes, some would also say the "unvirtue," the vice—in his own not fully examined soul devastated him.

Yet we read *Utopia* not to make fun of the "man for all seasons" who lost self-control, direction, and coherent philosophy when the season and spiritual climate changed. We revisit his book to get some sense of what ordered life can look like, and then to help point to present-day decisions as to what to rescue from More and to propose for elsewhere, especially in a religiously pluralist society. This is that reparative aspect of what Reinitz calls "humane irony" at work.

The Müntzer case displays the God-possessed ("enthusiastic") messianic community builder announcing that God would ensure protection and victory for the peasant forces, even if and maybe especially when they employ violent means. Yet when they acted, the heavens were silent; the promises Müntzer made were not able to be filled, and he was executed. It was folly to expect lightly armed peasants to use the idea of divine inspiration and protection in a self-described righteous but at all points futile cause. Müntzer had been too foolish, too lacking in virtue, too weak; his vision and the forces that produced disorder look foolish to us. It is hard at first to see how wisdom, virtue, strength, and prefigurings of order were a part of his ambiguous human mix.

Yet there are also good reasons not simply to deride Müntzer. He inspired secular movements that spread liberties and gave hope to peasants; he has been invoked in various liberation theology movements, be they completely nonviolent or ready for violence.

In the case of Andreae's *Christianopolis*, we find a vastly different approach to the way people should live together. Instead of using reason and the endeavors of humans, this Christian place, which remained only an on-paper place, was founded on precise, distinct, unmistakable, even propositional codes of revealed truth. Yet Andreae was not successful at showing how a biblical canon and scholastic structure as rigid as his could be welcoming, as he thought it would be, even to other Christian communions, to say nothing of other religious communities. And as Thomas More lost his life to the executioner, Andreae found his orthodox world, in this case Protestant versus Catholic, divided, its two halves at war. There was, to say the least, in the end and despite some appearances, nothing of tolerance or order in the world Andreae would have guided to scholastic orthodoxy and faith in God.

Yet one need not merely laugh in the what-fools-these-mortals-be spirit at Andreae's kind of endeavor. From his time until now, utopian communities and proposals are founded by people who bring explicit and defined outlooks. Yet some of them have learned to achieve what Andreae only dreamed of. One thinks of the American colonies of Rhode Island and Pennsylvania, founded by articulate Baptists in one case and convinced Quakers in the other. Both welcomed a variety of peoples who brought different Christianities and different faiths—beginning with Jews at Newport. Citizens at neither place found the search for order or the impulse to plan to be inhibiting. The humane ironic stance lets us see people such as Andreae in some positive light.

THE HUMANIST UTOPIA: THOMAS MORE'S TOLERANCE AND INTOLERANCE

Utopia, which many would say is literarily the best and also the most influential of the written utopias, gave the name to the genre and to endeavors patterned after such literature. No other work since Plato's *Republic* has had such lasting effect or served more regularly as a paradigm or measure for others. The author, Thomas More, later sainted by Catholicism, is known in contemporary America as "a man for all seasons," thanks to a biography and film that made him a familiar figure to moderns. In his time, monarchs alternated between commitments to Roman Catholicism, headed by the pope, and Anglican Catholicism, whose head was England's sovereign himself or herself. Those who rose in the ranks of state or church or both were vulnerable to the lethal consequence of betting on the wrong version of creed and authority at any particular time. Thomas More sent one set of dissenters to their death and, in a cruel but easy-to-comprehend turn of fate, suffered death as a dissenter himself.

Most utopian works beg to be read first of all as indictments of the existing culture or at least as marks of restlessness with its norms and practices. *Utopia,* the model for others, is no exception. The entire little book can be read as a critique of More's England, its state and church and economy. In that sense it is a disguised prophetic work of the sort that allows the author to be searching in a greater number of safe ways than if he simply issued a blast at things as they were.

Every commentator on *Utopia* has to reckon with one obvious and then one complex dimension. First, More used his fictive device to declaim against the flaws of all-too-real, nonutopian England. Almost every favorable feature of *Utopia* is the obverse of some social practice in the nation at the time. Second, on the positive side, when these favorable features appear, the reader or interpreter is hard pressed to know whether the real Thomas More is standing up or whether he is playing games and making fun while offering implicit proposals that he himself would not stand behind. Again, that aspect is what makes *Utopia* appear at times to be a flatly obvious book but more often a tantalizing riddle.

In it the hero, Raphael Hythlodae (translation: "nonsense-dispenser") sounds like a modern social critic, someone who would provoke agitation from those who would see him as a bleeding heart because he looked at societal situations and not at the evil in the thief's heart.

After that critical first part, More moved on to describe the positive features of his utopia: not void, not "no place," but a happy community, established to be permanent. Now we learn more about the island of Utopia. Utopus, the founder, having conquered the land he came across, undertook a huge digging project to sever it from the mainland. Conveniently, such sundering helped create an island, a better place for social experiment. It was to keep invaders away.

The economy and the family are two social elements that all utopians have to address, criticize, and seek to reform. More scoops up the family whole out of medieval settings. Father rules, patriarchally; the cousins are an extension of this unity; the family is the producer and central economic force. Wives have to be subordinate to their husbands; this utopia is not a feminist's dream. Before festivals, wives have to kneel before their husbands, as do children before their parents, asking forgiveness for their faults and sins. There are slaves; More is not picturing their abolition even in Utopia.

One feature of Utopian life would strike the modern democrat as bearing the marks of the authoritarian state: The magistrates could invade the privacy of all and have their eyes out for any deviations from the permissible. Hythlodae noted that everyone worked when work was scheduled because no one escaped the watchful eyes of the magistrates. And where could one hide from scrutiny? Nowhere. More's Utopia banned taverns, brothels, and any "secret meeting places" where there could be seductions.

Where did Utopians get slaves? From the cohort of punished citizens, by borrowing criminals from elsewhere, or by just plain asking for them or paying a pittance. When moderns of republican instincts speak of utopia in positive terms, they have to know that More's version would have kept Amnesty International busy.

One would have expected More the Christian to measure humanity in terms of the early chapters of the book of Genesis. Yet he did not picture his community as a reversion to Eden, as so many primitivist utopians were later to do. His Utopians were morally responsible individuals but not paradisiacal angels. This was not a second paradise but a place where "the crooked timber of humanity" was building something straight. Utopia provided straightening, not because humans were so naturally good but because the laws and provisions were.

Thus—we turn for this to the Niebuhrian quadrilateral of ironic elements—More, the drafter of this utopia, showed some awareness of the vice that exists within and alongside human virtues, the weaknesses inside the strengths, the insecurity shrouded under apparent security, the folly that lurks under the surface of wisdom—to which we now add the disorder that utopian order was supposed to disguise and transform. Hence his utopian project seemed at first glance to be protected from features that evoke ironic interpretation. And since More's Utopia never had to be or got to be founded, built, and inhabited, the shambles it would have produced never appeared.

Despite those safeguards, to which More's ironic literary style contributed, there were still ironies in his interpretation of the good life and community. The search for order has motivated much, probably most, of utopian writing. And the disorder that it sets out to overcome but which instead overcomes the efforts is a characteristic element to be noticed in ironic perspective. Doris Donnelly comments on this: "What is most significant . . . is that in *Utopia* More departs not only from the predominant medieval idea that the natural order is defined according to a theory of divine order, but also from the prevailing classical notion that the natural order is the result of our understanding of a supertemporal realm of order, a transcendent realm of order which is the source of order in the phenomenal world." By More's time the search for order had become focused less on the foundations of the medieval church and more on the emerging state and the political order. "This new notion of order, with its focus on the creation of an ideal state that directs humankind toward the attainment of the good life in this world, informs this most famous of all 'well-ordered commonwealths,'" his Utopia.

Having taken the requisite tour of his Utopia, we have until now left out features that loom large in our interpretation and More's legacy. More is regarded as passionate and committed to whatever version of Christianity was his option at particular times in England, yet Utopia was not a set of Christian city-states. It anticipated the more benign versions of the Enlightenment's "reasonable" religion. Hythlodae observed quietly and casually that divine revelation was denied the Utopians. They listened to reason and, following a favored philosophy of the day, worked by deduction as they came to see and follow the divine way. Some call this Christian's utopia "pagan"; I prefer to call it humanistic, or religiously humanistic.

Someone familiar with the reputation of Thomas More as a heresy hunter is likely to come up short as Hythlodae comes to a climax: "Finally, let me tell you about their religious ideas. There are several different religions on the island, and indeed in each town. There are sun worshippers, moon worshippers and worshippers of various other planets," he began his catalog. "There are people who regard some great or good man of the past not merely as a god, but as the supreme god. However, the vast majority take the much more sensible view that there is a single divine power, unknown, eternal, infinite, inexplicable and quite beyond the grasp of the human mind, diffused throughout this universe of ours, not as a physical substance but as an active force. This power they call 'The Parent.'" Shades of gender-inclusive religious language that for nonutopians of the West was still centuries in the offing! In respect to this Parent: "They give Him credit for everything that happens to everything, for all beginnings and ends, all growth, development, and change. Nor do they recognize any other form of deity." And "On this point, indeed, all the different sects agree—that there is one Supreme Being, Who is responsible for the creation and management of the Universe." This Being gets the Utopian name Mythras.

Continuing with surprises and shocks, More also saw women joining men as priests in these religions. Nor did they become priests by appointment from above. The people elected them, as they could not in Catholicism or Anglicanism in More's real world.

More could not refrain from picturing that these good religions were close to Christianity; indeed, as Hythlodae pictured them, they were poised to become part of it. As a matter of fact, while visiting Utopia, More had Hythlodae and companions baptizing some, but then having to abandon them to reason instead of nurturing them through the sacraments, because there were no Christian priests on the scene.

More's own "real" world, in which he participated with zest and zeal, was made up of people who fought over religion as dispensed, monitored, and regulated by pope and crown, bishop and prince, priest and magistrate in an elaborate hierarchical and sacramental system. He was to die for his commitment to one side in the debates. Yet when he envisioned Utopia he anticipated both some Protestant Reformation and then Enlightenment understandings of the nature, place, and relation of religions. On the island a kind of moralistic faith prevailed, one that later Anglican latitudinarians and deists could favor but Catholics could not.

The whole passage about tolerant generalized religion could seem to be the product of one of those ironic twists in More's style; was he pulling our leg and divorcing himself entirely from his own utopia? Not likely, since Hythlodae went on to point to a congruence compatible with his Catholicism: "But when we told [the Utopians] about Christ, His teaching, His character, His miracles, and the no less miraculous devotion of all the martyrs who, by voluntarily shedding their blood, converted so many nations to the Christian faith, you've no idea how easy it was to convert them." Why? "Perhaps it was because Christianity seemed so very like their own principal religion—though I should imagine they were also considerably affected by the information that Christ prescribed of His own disciples a communist way of life, which is still practised today in all the most truly Christian communities. Anyway, whatever the explanation, quite a lot of Utopians adopted our religion, and were baptised."

Thomas More, ironically, did not find it possible to take lessons from his own book when his time of testing came. Not many years after he wrote this prescription for tolerance he ground up others and then was ground up himself in conflict over intolerant, torturing creedal faiths. The author of *Utopia* could not have met the standards of his own utopia, could not have lived there, and, by all evidence, would not have wanted to, preferring as he did the dogmatic and absolutist approach to faith. His commentators and biographers have difficulty with this contradictory element, and some find ways to harden the edges of his description of tolerance in *Utopia* and explain some of the reasons for his intolerance as heresy hunter.

Even a brief survey of *Utopia* in fairness has to include reference to the disjunction between book and author, or between early More and late More, especially in an essay like this one on the ironic perspective. Thus translator Paul Turner footnotes this subject: "There seems to be no doubt that More sentenced some people to death (which meant burning alive) for heresy, and in one late letter he unembarrassedly admitted that he had said, in respect to Protestants, that Christ is personally responsible for the burning of heretics. "I would some good friend of [Protestant John Frith] would show him, that I fear me sore that *Christ will kindle a fire of faggots for him,* and make him therein sweat the blood out of his body here" [italics Turner's]. Explain it away as one will, Turner says, "a certain inconsistency remains, and no humane person who otherwise admires More can help being horrified to find him taking such a very un-Utopian line in real life."

Where once More had wanted to tease and provoke, later he wanted to injure and destroy. Where in *Utopia* he could earlier "praise folly" by ridiculing the self-important and pointing to flaws in the legal system or the habits of clergy, later these were themselves violent agents to be used against More himself. The Niebuhrian ironist might have said, in the spirit of Psalm 2:4, that the God who sits in the heavens could laugh at the pretensions of people such as More. And yet this laughing God would also hold such people responsible and would honor their aspirations.

More could not have foreseen the many uses to which *Utopia* would be put. Historians track his influence among communists, socialists, imperialists, democrats, medievalists, Catholic hagiographers (who tend to slide past the book to get to the "real" More), revolutionaries, individualists, capitalists, humanists, satirists, existentialists, and structuralists, among others.

While the later Thomas More is not of the barrel-of-laughs sort, I find it in place to end this account of More with reference to his death. Paul Turner in a footnote offers a snapshot of it, on which biographers enlarge. An early life, by Sir William Roper, has More going up the scaffold, which was so weak that it was ready to fall, and saying merrily to the master lieutenant: "Help me up with your hand, for as for my comming doone, let me shift as I may, for by then I ame sure I shall take no greate harme." After this review of the ironic outcome of More's endeavor, there comes the time to say, "But even so, look at that!" I argue that there is still incentive to human aspiration, even if God has laughed first, if one revisits *Utopia* and rescues from the author and his time some clues for ways in which people of commitment can also display tolerance of the sort that the author himself in the end could not.

THE RADICAL UTOPIA: THOMAS MÜNTZER'S VIOLENT KINGDOM

Thomas Müntzer's utopia was never to be realized, but the struggle to attain it belonged to the very real world of violent writing, preaching, and revolt among people of different faiths, classes, and situations, even though its author professed to be seeking a kingdom of peace. Both have had an influence on subsequent aspirations toward forming "the perfect society." Müntzer (born 1488 or 1489, died 1525) one of the most prominent radical leaders in the Protestant Reformation during its formative decade on the European continent, qualifies as a utopian. He envisioned and worked to produce a kind of city and kingdom that was qualitatively different from what existed in Europe in his time. He was a pioneer among those who preached modern religious utopias, though he left no blueprint for his. A visionary, a dreamer, and a person of action, he set out to transcend the existing boundaries of personal and communal life in the German territories of his day. While his militant efforts led to early defeat and to his own death, and while no Müntzerian communities came to be established, Müntzer lives on as a pathfinder on the radical reform front and has deserved much scholarly attention in our own time.

His was an endeavor to foresee and contribute to the fashioning of a perfect society. Perfect does not mean that all its citizens would transcend the boundaries of human existence or, in Reformation-era terms, that they would be exempt from original sin. It does mean that the framework of this future realm would be purged of those elements that by definition and position stood in the way of the purposes of God. Müntzer advocated what some call the first Protestant theocracy, a God-ruled state. There had been theocracies, of course, long before the sixteenth century, and often elsewhere than Germany. None of these mattered more to the biblicist Müntzer than that of ancient Israel, his prototype. The cleric knew his Bible and recognized clearly from study of it that the people of Israel were flawed. Their covenant, he knew, was perfect, but they often violated it. Similarly, the governance of the primitive Christian church was a model for him. From the biblical book of Acts he could well recognize the flaws among the apostolic followers of Jesus themselves. Yet he dreamed that the communities of Allstedt and Mühlhausen in sixteenth-century Germany could draw from and improve upon the primitive Christian paradigm in their pursuit of the ideal community and rule.

Second, to say that God was the direct source of rule does not mean that God needed no human mediator or instrument. Utopians cannot take chances on leadership by uncertain or in other ways inadequate mediators. By seeing himself as God's prophet, his latter-day Daniel, Müntzer wanted to assure those who would benefit from the new way of living that they could have confidence about the future. We customarily recognize utopian inventors as self-assured, charismatic, and bold in their designs. When one of them sees himself as God's instrument—a role countless later utopians would also assign themselves—we can score the utopian intention as having been firm.

Third among the marks that renders Müntzer's prophetic vision utopian was his idea that, in a model of early Christians as pictured in the book of Acts, the saints were to hold all things in common.

A fourth feature that marks Müntzer's envisioned communities of reform as utopian relates to the fact that he saw this model as having universal application. Wherever the pure Word of God was to be preached, heard, and followed, the people would live in a new kind of circumstance. Müntzer's utopia was therefore more defined and radical than most, since so many other utopians did not picture that the whole world might follow them, or did not see a need to put to the sword those who rejected the opportunity to join the elect. And few utopians reached as far as Müntzer did in speaking of the new status of the elect in his utopia. He preached that thanks to the incarnation of God in Christ, fleshly, earthly people should become gods and thus disciples with Him. They would be *vergöttet*—made divine because of His teaching. This meant that they should be utterly transformed in the process, and terrestrial life would begin to become a heaven. So Müntzer was engaged neither in mere backward-looking "restitution" of the apostolic church nor in becoming a Marxist type of revolutionary. After the German revolution of 1848 Friedrich Engels recalled the Peasants' War of 1525 and Müntzer, who sided with the peasants, as prefigurings of the Marxist-type revolutions that were to come. While the churches had little to do with the Müntzer legacy, Engels would say that Müntzer's political doctrine extended as far beyond the existing social and political conditions as his theology surpassed the ideas valid for his time. Müntzer was a God-intoxicated reformer who claimed to be moved by the very Spirit of God repudiated by the twentieth-century atheistic regime in East Germany, which often claimed him.

Müntzer was a member of the first generation of university-bred Germans who grew restless with the Catholic expression and institutions of the day. In his formative years and until Martin Luther disappointed and then ruthlessly attacked him, Müntzer idolized and quoted and corresponded with that reformer. He was trying to remake Luther in an image congenial to his own endeavors, not realizing that the two were far apart in theology and certainly in strategic understandings.

Müntzer was not a scholar's scholar, someone who would be content to pursue humanist ideas of reform in the study. Yet he was scholarly, well-read, and never a mere activist. He could read Latin, Greek, and Hebrew. The young reformer was informed by the writings of the thirteenth-century visionary and Franciscan monk Joachim de Fiore, the inspirer of so many dreamers of apocalypse who envisioned new orders of the world. Müntzer was particularly well-read in the mystics, some of them from the recent German past. He drew much from the legacy of the remarkable abbess and mystic Hildegard of Bingen. Through his acquaintance with such he began to feel free to speak of his own direct experiences of God. This was something that the scripture-centered Lutheran leaders would not do. So Müntzer took on Luther directly in a tract of 1524 after the two had broken.

Müntzer charged that Luther had misrepresented him and made fun of him by saying that the radical heard angels speak to him. Müntzer replied that he praised God for doing what God wanted with him, as he preached the Bible, not his own ideas. Above all, and however much Müntzer felt the closeness of the divine Spirit, he was also a scripturalist. As with many utopians, he had some sense that the movements he encouraged were prescribed. He used prophetic books and gospels to spell out the redemptive character of suffering.

Müntzer had briefly supervised a nunnery before Luther recommended him for appointment to a pulpit in Zwickau, a town of weavers and miners who, it turns out, were ready for radical preaching. Their new pastor attacked ruling powers in church and state at once, thereby becoming an embarrassment to moderate reformers. He attacked priests and monks in a Christmas sermon in 1520. The sermon stirred up a mob against a cleric Müntzer had criticized. When pressed, he justified the call to violence. The town leadership expelled him and dispersed his followers.

Staying on the trail of Müntzer is always rather difficult. His restlessness of soul was the internal expression of a way of life that has to be described as peregrinating. Saying that he wanted to gain the ear of the entire world for the sake of the word, he made his way around Bohemia, then also in throes of reform-versus-antireform activity. He came to Prague, where he linked up with Czech and Bohemian reform elements that drew on the legacy of Jan Hus, who had been martyred by the Council of Constance a century earlier. While in Prague, with a histrionic touch that emulated Luther's posting of the Ninety-five Theses four years to the day earlier, he posted a document addressed to clergy and humanists, on All Saints' Day 1521. It has come to be called the *Prague Manifesto*. The manifesto did make clear Müntzer's messianic self-concept. He located himself as successor to the "dear and holy crusader John Hus" and proclaimed himself the one who would inaugurate the next, last age of the world. Then God could act and create a place and time in which the elect would live as Adam and Eve had before the Fall. And he charged peasants not to let their swords grow cold, urging them to strike the anvil with the hammer. No wonder the Prague officials forbade Müntzer from preaching such disturbing, even disrupting words; he was arrested and banished in late 1521.

Regularly Müntzer, as utopian, spoke of changing the world by renewing the church. He described a poor, miserable, pitiful, and wretched Christendom, which through spiritual adultery had become a harlot. He was sure that God had a plan for history and that in his time he was God's instrument to fulfill it. Unlike More and Andreae, he made up the details of his utopia as he went along. One wonders what would have happened had the revolt been successful and a Müntzerian polity had been set up anywhere—and he been called upon to run it.

Like many a utopian activist, Müntzer found it ever more necessary to sweep widely and cut deeply. After he somehow gained another appointment, perhaps at the hands of a woman of the nobility who admired him, he located in Allstedt, a major base of operations for him in his brief years. There he made a second utopian's move by encouraging the development of a group he called the Bund, a gathering of the elect. This was a cabal or cadre, largely secret, called to capture his central idea and then engage in violent action.

Exactly what the Bund was up to has never been made clear, though some said it was started so that people could stay true to God and his gospel. Not much came of the Bund practically, especially when the Peasants' War began. It had served symbolic purposes in the reformer's prerevolt sermons.

In the short term, however, and whatever the longer program was to have been, some of the Bund's members acted. They attacked a chapel, a symbol of authority in places such as Allstedt. They also savaged a shrine, such holy places being symbols of the piety of those the attackers saw as spiritually enslaved. Müntzer defended their action in terms that have to be described as overly self-assured, righteous. Rather naively, given all he had said to this point, and per-haps overly confident in his own preacherly ability to change people, he beckoned to the prince to sign up for his elect association of true believers. If the civil leaders would not do so, he threatened that he would appeal to the poor lay folk and the peasants.

The preaching grew ever more radical, especially in Müntzer's repeated call for the killing of princes, priests, or anyone who stood in the way of the Holy Spirit and this reformer. The good princes must attack and purge the evil ones. They must drive out God's enemies; they were the means for it. If the ungodly stood in the way of the pious, they had no right to live.

In July of 1524 Duke John gave signs that he was getting the point of the now-subversive messages that had never been uttered too discreetly. To see how Müntzer had lost perspective, one need only examine the scene when Duke John and his son Frederick came to look into things and heard Müntzer, who of course knew they were in the congregation, preach on the prophet Daniel. While such preaching had to be designed against the nobles' kind of authority and rule, Müntzer naively or in messianic spirit invited the nobles to come into the community he was envisioning and programming. They were not impressed.

It was time for Müntzer to get out of town, which he did by climb-ing a wall and scrambling away. He was not always on the battle lines, where courage was required. While Luther was making his stand at the Diet of Worms, Müntzer explained his absence from the scene of conflict with an alibi: "I was in the bath at the time." Soon he was setting out, urging along the scheme that would move his people to their utopian adventure, known to history as the Peasants' War. He did not instigate or lead it, but he supported and exploited it when it broke out. On March 17, 1525, Müntzer and allies helped recruit fighters and prepare weapons. A banner appeared for battle, white with a rainbow on it: *Verbum domini maneat in eternum* (the Word of God will remain forever). It hung behind the altar at St. Mary's church, but was also readied for battle use.

Battles were soon to come as peasants, squeezed by changes in culture and commerce, were cramped between the feudal economy of barter and the emerging economy of money. The owners of property exacted ever more produce as rent and tribute from them. Unquestionably they had profound grievances. And they had begun to hear the language of liberation from Luther himself. But when violence came, Luther stood back from the revolt and sided with the princes while Müntzer plunged in. Almost at once the princes were in command against outnumbered, underorganized peasants with meager weapons.

Müntzer identified in extreme fashion with the peasants, signing off his legitimations of rebellion and revolt with the words "with the sword of Gideon." This was a reference to a military leader of God's ancient chosen people, as Müntzer read history. It was one more sign that he had worked for transformation of existing society and with transcendent appeals to governing all the way. Now he had reached the point where boundaries between God and human, Spirit and Müntzer, had been dissolved.

Those who fought the princes were outnumbered and outarmed, with less competent leaders, so nothing but disaster followed for the peasants, as there was no divine rescue. Preparing for battle, the peasants created a barricade of wagons that of course turned out to be no defense at all. Five thousand were killed, hundreds were captured, some escaped. On the other side, only six of the princes' men died.

During the bloodbath Müntzer, who had long offered his life willingly for God's cause, lost courage. Enemies found him feigning illness, hidden in bed in an attic at Frankenhausen in May of 1525. Captured, he was brought to trial and tortured. Then came the disgrace such leaders most abhor: the collapse of his inner resistance. The nature and circumstances of his recantation will remain mysteriously shrouded. Was his word given voluntarily? Did he write it all? He confessed in writing that he had incited this rebellion so that all Christendom should be equal and that the lords and nobles who do not stand by the gospel should be killed.

Müntzer recanted his violent revolutionary teachings, but too late. The victors executed him with fifty-three other partisans after he had pleaded on May 27, 1525, that the peasants should lay down their weapons and come to terms for peace. Finally, with the rebellion over, Luther began to put in good words for the peasants and their causes. Once more: too late.

Müntzer never did get to set up the kingdom on earth that he pictured being governed by the gospel. There is no statement of his teachings comparable to the explicit envisioning in More's *Utopia* or Andreae's *Christianopolis*. Instead we have snippets and snapshots, but certainly enough to go on to see what he was envisioning.

Irony? In Müntzer's case there was enough vice barely hidden in his virtue, which had been directed to improving the situation of peasants; enough weakness to compromise his strength, as he failed to lead effectively and sought protection in the end; enough insecurity to jostle him out of security because he placed reliance on a hidden God who never promised to become overt and to protect his cause; enough folly to displace the wisdom of the scholar's early years; enough disorder in the chaos of the peasants' revolt to make one forget that the whole preachment was designed to produce a new order.

The perspective of humane irony prompts the intervention now, "But even so, look at this!" The Marxists, Christians pushed to extremes of violence, and even some nonviolent Christians who wanted to identify with those outcast and abused, have snatched from Müntzer's words and record elements that inspire them still to challenge oppressors—in some cases, at least, with more clarity and modesty than Müntzer could evidence.

THE ORTHODOX UTOPIA: JOHANN ANDREAE'S ORDER

The third of our midmillennium utopias was a purely literary project, never rendered into community or bricks and wood, and never intended to be thus realized by its author. That visionary was Johann Valentin Andreae, an imitator of and a lesser German counterpart to Thomas More. Andreae was typical of utopians in expressing his self-assuredness as he set about writing in detail his vision of the perfect society. It was part of a program to help Germans bridge from the times we now call the Reformation toward the new age of science that came to be known as the Enlightenment.

If More's pride was cushioned and tempered by his irony, Andreae, not incapable of expressing himself with ironic wit, shows only a trace of it in his utopian book. He admitted that since he did not like to be corrected, he "built" this city for himself so he could exercise dictatorship. And he demonstrated the chutzpah utopians need to venture forth and give a rationale for writing. The style of Andreae's *Christianopolis,* more properly *Rei publicae Christiano-politanae Descriptio,* and the fact that this *descriptio* was not acted upon any more than More's *Utopia* ever got to be founded, renders him somewhat less available to the ironic perspective than was Thomas

Müntzer. Just as some utopians offered ideas that practical people could employ in many another kind of polis, so other utopian writers could take ideas from communities that already embodied some elements of what utopians seek. Thus before Andreae wrote he visited Geneva, Switzerland, where a more ordered version of the Reformation than the Lutheran or Anabaptist had taken shape. Obedience to civil authority guided by God's book and people meant that those who lived under it could be assured of absolute guidance, as if God were directly in command.

Andreae came on that scene wanting to celebrate science, as his *Christianopolis* certainly did. He wanted to be at home in the three worlds of religious orthodoxy, science, and magic, whether he would always call them that or not. And the citizens of *Christianopolis* were also to be given to the three, though religious orthodoxy curiously received least attention and seemed subject to most revision among them.

Lutherans have not often made very good utopians before or after that curious generation in which Andreae integrated witness to Christ with the physical sciences. Central for him was the presence of the eternal Logos made flesh, Jesus Christ. In that combination Christianopolitans would live in an ideal Lutheran society. Andreae's "city" was to be a *paradigma*, something that when thus named does not have to be perfectly realized.

Let us go along with the author in his conceit that his was an entertainment, a Thomas Morean *ludicrum*, in the form of a travel tale. At times Andreae seemed eager to show off, at others to elicit chuckles, and at still others to make serious proposals without putting himself at much risk. As in the cases of fantasist More and preacher Müntzer, Andreae used his genre to blast the very nonutopian society he saw around him. His book appeared almost precisely at the time of the outbreak of the Thirty Years' War, and it reflected a society torn by Catholic-Protestant schism and corruption in church and state.

The author contributed to confusion by calling his dreamed-of place an *urbs, oppidum*, or *civitas* in his Latin version of 1619. But his families make up more of a domestic commune whose members do what monks do than a community of urbanites bustling around a city. The people are pictured as being so efficient in their light-industrial ways that there had to have been an oversupply of produce and products needing export, but Andreae spent no time working out that practical element. Because the author could never be quite clear in his mind, his intentions, and his writings, as to whether he was designing a kind of monastic refuge from and power center for the larger city-states or a potential city itself, he left himself vulnerable to the maze of interpretations that followed.

Andreae made so much of monastery-style discipline because his is a plot against disorder, a place that keeps visions of battle, famine, and suffering at a distance. In such a setting the citizens could spend their time in discourse on philosophical models—or they could go in pursuit of God and the divine vision. Scholars have an easy time of it treating the text of *Christianopolis* faithfully and following its sequences. Who but an author given to order and the integral would see to it that there would be exactly one hundred neatly organized chapters, "examinations" and "lectures" from which one can pick and choose.

Thus the creedal emphasis stands out. While More's *Utopia* allowed for various sorts of pious humanists, Andreae's plot had to sound Lutheranly orthodox. Thus in an astonishing scene, one that would be contrary to utopian impulse in almost any other writers, the visitor to Christianopolis comes across a double tablet with gold letters announcing the creed of the inhabitants. Paragraph II on the tablet comes straight out of the books of dogma, stated in Lutheran fashion. Yet he included an ecumenical vision, though most members of other religious bodies would have rejected his creed.

Andreae did not meet death by execution as More did. But he suffered from precisely the kinds of ills he would have purged from his utopia. He was a pastor in Vaihingen until 1620, where he met constant disputes, saw the corruption of morals, complained that he suffered slights and bitterness. He then moved on to Calw where the privations and dangers of the Thirty Years' War reached him. In 1634 he and his family had to flee the torched city in midwinter. One of his sons died from exposure to the cold during the flight.

His final position was at the Cloister School in Bebenhausen, where the would-be superorthodox visionary met constant charges of theological error, but he stayed with the work until bad health forced his retirement. He died in 1654. Posterity's judgment—there was some—could be friendly. The German pietists appreciated his critique of the established church. In the larger society, Leibniz recognized Andreae's provision for learning in society, Herder regarded him for his writing, and Goethe took inspiration from Andreae for the scene in the study in *Faust*. Yet he was generally forgotten and his writings are not part of the Western canon.

"But even so, look at that!" From the perspective of humane irony, these societies in which Andreae had a part suggested that while his utopia could not be anything more than an often futile imaginative construct, he hoped that readers would draw a sense of responsibility from it. Some things learned from his envisionings served him and his derivative successors in prototypical learned societies.

Ironically, the classical utopian who set out to ensure an airtight, dogmatic, permanent theological foundation for his community was not able to live out a life that exempted him from the disorder he would flee. What legacy he left was snatched and transformed, as we have seen, by the likes of those he would have dismissed as heterodox: Leibniz and Herder and Goethe, the pioneers of Enlightenment and Romantic unorthodoxies. These were still somehow stirred, if in always and only those heterodox ways, by something dreamed of and sketched in *Christianopolis.*

AGAIN: "EVEN SO, LOOK AT THAT. . ."

Kenneth M. Roemer makes the point in *The Obsolete Necessity* that utopias and America-as-utopia are "obsolete," but the utopian venture merits study, he adds. He quotes Lewis Mumford: "We can never reach the points of the compass [the utopian poles]; and so no doubt we shall never live in Utopia; but without the magnetic needle we should not be able to travel intelligently at all." That suggestion is on the hyperbolic side, which is where Mumford liked to reside, but it offers a clue that we can follow more cautiously. Roemer contends that, "rapid, multidimensional change accompanied by a desire for simplicity, unity, and order are, if anything, more characteristic of the twentieth than of the nineteenth century" as he makes the case for *The Obsolete Necessity.* "Therefore the earlier Utopian works can provide insights into the roots of such problems and reactions to them." So, I would argue, can other utopias, such as those offered in the centuries during the breakup of Christendom and the coming of the Enlightenment and many periods since.

Having raided Roemer for the idea of "the obsolete necessity," it would be unfair not to let him have a last word. I find it a bit exaggerated, in the mood of Mumford, but we listen: "Of course, speculating about bringing the good life to everyone and ideals that make daily existence meaningful is a frustrating—'Utopian'—venture. Moreover, today it calls for a pluralistic idealism quite foreign to late nineteenth-century Utopianism. But consider the alternative: drifting from expedient to ad hoc buoyed only by piecemeal reforms and fragmented values that are out of touch with much of our everyday experience. Some ingredients of Utopianism are ridiculously, even cruelly, obsolete; but now, more than ever, discovering Utopia is a necessity." Those last five words strike me as, yes, utopian. But "discovering Utopia" or "learning from failed Utopias and adaptations that followed their experiments" can be a profitable venture, one of many instruments to be used by realists who write scenarios and make plans for varieties of futures.

Here we have been interested in asking what has been durable in the utopian impulse in the West, an impulse that is likely to persist. We began with Isaiah Berlin on the limits of the utopias he never fully rejected, and he here gets penultimate place. What has been a problem through utopian writing is not that authors dreamed, used imagination, or had the courage required to write scenarios or build settings for the future. The problem arose because, in their search for order, utopians have tended to be too sure of the integrality of the whole, the unity of the outcome. Here Berlin attacks: "This unifying monistic pattern is at the very heart of the traditional rationalism, religious and atheistic, metaphysical and scientific, transcendental and naturalistic, that has been characteristic of Western civilization. Berlin placed the writers of Utopias from More onward among them."

Whether philosophically based, in the tradition of Thomas More; rooted in revolutionary visions based on claims of direct divine revelation, as with Thomas Müntzer; or seeking ordered outcome based on orthodoxies of the sort Johann Andreae favored, Berlin's point stands:

"All the Utopias known to us are based upon the discoverability and harmony of objectively true ends, true for all men, at all times and in all places," from Plato through the "Utopias of Thomas More and Campanella, Bacon and Harrington and Fenelon." These all rest, he says, on "the three pillars of social optimism in the West of which I have spoken: that the central problems—the *massimi problemi*—of men are, in the end, the same throughout history; that they are in principle soluble; and that the solutions form a harmonious whole."

Because the utopians forget that humans and their endeavors are "crooked timbers," their efforts fail. But some of them fail interestingly, and their failures can inspire the imagination of those who retrieve some positive and often practical elements from their writings and experimental communities and plans. There are reasons to include them in intellectual histories of the West and in practical planning, in the spirit that says when things go wrong, "But even so, look at that!"

The final word comes from our revisiting of Reinhold Niebuhr, the theologian who reintroduced above the utopian scene of the God who laughs when "the people imagine a vain thing." The divine laugh and the human echo do not have to be the last word: For Niebuhr and other believers in such a God, the point is to witness to the larger culture that the "whole drama of human history is under the scrutiny of a divine judge who laughs at human pretensions without being hostile to human aspirations." There, "if the laughter is truly ironic it must symbolize mercy as well as judgment. For whenever judgment defines the limits of human striving it creates the possibility of an humble acceptance of . . . limits. Within that humility mercy and peace find a lodging place." The historical record suggests that it may be as much an imagination of a "vain thing" to foreclose that possibility as it has been, among Utopians, to make too much of it.

POSTSCRIPT: LEARNING FROM EXPERIENCE: A CASE STORY

I was once involved in a quasi-utopian experiment, an experience that informs my thesis. It was called Minnesota Experimental City, or MXC, the brainchild of an admired friend, the late Otto A. Silha, chair and publisher of the Minneapolis Star and Tribune Company. That it was not able to be developed and in the eyes of its critics looked like one more failed utopia is a factor in its favor, in respect to our purposes. Nonetheless, I would not waste a reader's time telling any part of its story if failure were the only feature of its plot. I tell it because it illustrates something of what can come of practical utopian thought.

Otto Silha sought to help the leadership ensure that humanist concerns would be present in the planning of a city for which technological addresses to problems were prime. And the plan? The proposal was to build "an entirely new city which would serve as a national proving ground for social, economic, and technological innovation." Part of the language about that city held that it would represent an experimental "overleap" by planners who had lost patience with plodding, compromising, urban endeavors that were far from any kind of leaping.

"Overleap," they wrote, "is used here to mean at once an advance into future possibilities and a break with past constraints." Aware that others might call MXC a pure utopia, the planners pointed out that through "continuing experimentation," it would be a proving ground and thus presumably should not fall under the kind of scrutiny the scornful give Utopias. Still, it was to be a "total systems experiment," the description of a pursuit of ordering that again comes fairly close to what many critics do call Utopia. The reporting committee italicized the point: *A new city is essential because only there would a total systems experiment be possible.*

In its development, as MXC's report of 1969 contended, was an "opportunity to start anew without those entangling restrictions which impair the visibility of our cities today. In short, for the first time in the history of man, we are seeking to build a whole new city from an ecological base." It would be a project "to transform research and technology into reality." MXC would combine energies of industries and corporations connected with Minnesota, a branch of the state university, and other enterprises.

The MXC report sets forth that "the City has as its premise that: (1) man can creatively mold his environment; (2) that he can, in a positive and constructive way, unite the resources of private technology with public authority; and that (3) he can reorient social, economic, and physical forces to serve people." But Silha and company asked questions like these in respect to the human element: "What will be man's reaction to proposed innovations? How long and how extensively will he accept innovation, and what will be its effect on his desire for evolutionary change and his innate reluctance to accept revolutionary change?"

Cautionary words showed how careful we planners were not to be typed as utopians: "An important potential limitation is our inability to predict human reactions to it as a place to live." And most urgent of all: "Involved in these questions regarding men's values and desired living arrangements are perhaps the largest constraints of all to the realization of the Experimental City." No true utopianism there, either. At quarterly meetings scientists, businesspeople, educators, politicians, and humanists faced up to problems of human scale; the "location" of senior citizens, the absence or presence of a ghetto, the question of ennui that could accompany the realization.

The more we raised such questions, the more we came to remind ourselves that we did not have good answers and could not know where to go to find them. There well might never be good answers. So the humanist issues that had seemed like luxuries to be raised and discussed by MXC leaders soon occupied center stage, and technology kept its happy home in the "no problem" sectors of utopia. One contributor to the end of the experiment was the failure of Minnesotan Hubert Humphrey to win the presidency. In the Nixon administration, Vice President Spiro T. Agnew was assigned the approach to cities. He hated their disorder and, it was rumored, liked MXC too much; it was ordered. In any case, the city was never built. "But even so, look at that!"

The efforts had not been without product. From the frustrated planning, Otto Silha and his colleagues brought forth City Innovation: A Volunteer Non-Profit Program for America's Future, a venture that has survived beyond its third decade. Its original advisory board included numbers of people who took lessons from the imaginative work that went into MXC. Elements that had looked promising in that unrealized city now informed the efforts of those who dealt with real cities.

Matters of education and blue-collar jobs that were central to MXC planners decades earlier became the focus of later programs. In the last year of his life, Silha pointed to an Executives in Schools program in New York City that was beginning to attract support from some principals and retired executives. In Chicago, a "trifecta" program, "Blue Collar Jobs," worked to help young people cross "the digital divide" and get better jobs in the information age. For several years, earlier in the 1990s, the team came up with ideas for "The Crescent Corridor," a half-moon-shaped slice of Chicago-area lakeside life, ideas that would help revitalize a spent industrial area.

You had not heard about these? They are not large factors on the urban scene? Local officials have not picked up on enough of them? Others come up with programs like these without having precedents in envisioned MXCs? Skeptical questions are very much in place. And one would not want to claim too much for any program snatched after something goes wrong. But it is in such circumstances as these that new ideas with practical implications emerge in a nation that needs more of such. Berlin, again: "Utopias have their value—nothing so wonderfully expands the imaginative horizons of human potentialities."

INDEX